Le Lys d'Or

THE CHATEAUX OF FRANCE

CHATEAU-GAILLARD

THE CHATEAUX
OF FRANCE

FRANÇOIS GEBELIN

Translated by H. EATON HART

LONDON · ERNEST BENN LIMITED

First published in this edition 1964 by Ernest Benn Limited
Bouverie House · Fleet Street · London · EC4

© *1964 by Ernest Benn Limited and G. P. Putnam's Sons*

Translated from the French, 'Les Châteaux de France'

© *Presses Universitaires de France 1962*

Text printed in Great Britain · Illustrations printed in France

| CONTENTS

| LIST OF ILLUSTRATIONS

tower itself) date most probably from the beginning of the fifteenth century. The small tower with a conical roof in the centre of the building houses a spiral staircase. The low towers standing in the water on the left cover a system of three drawbridges crossing the moat. (Lapie. Photothèque française.) *facing p.* 48

PLATE V

THE CASTLE, TARASCON. The castle, which is in a remarkable state of preservation, is a quadrilateral flanked by four towers, of which the two overlooking the Rhône are square, the other two (overlooking the town), round. As at the Bastille, the top of the towers is at the same level as the top of the curtains, thus allowing uninterrupted movement along the wall-walk. The bailey-wall, with its two square towers, can be seen on the right, beyond the bridge. (Photothèque française.) *facing p.* 49

PLATE VI

AZAY-LE-RIDEAU. The photograph is taken from the south-east and shows the southern façade overlooking the River Indre. It will be seen that the middle bay of the façade has twice the width of the others, the reason being that it houses the staircase. The right-hand turret on the smaller (eastern) façade is modern. (Giraudon.) *facing p.* 54

PLATE VII

THE KEEP, VINCENNES. The quadrilateral plan with round corner towers denotes a reaction against the circular keeps introduced by Phillip-Augustus. An interesting feature – and an innovation at that time – is the double (superimposed) wall-walk, which was originally crenellated. The wall-walk on the chemise has alternate square openings and arrow-loops, and machicolations mounted on consoles (all of which have been preserved). On the gatehouse, however, and on the look-out towers at the corners the crenellations have disappeared. (Ciccione-Rapho.) *facing p.* 64

PLATE VIII

LE PLESSIS-BOURRÉ. Jean Bourré acquired the domain of 'Plessis-le-Vent' on November 26th, 1462. The castle must have been nearing completion on January 14th, 1472, when a contract was signed for the glass required for the openings. The photograph shows the outer façade of the main building (which houses the living quarters) and the keep at the south-east (right-hand) corner. (Boudot-Lamotte.) *facing p.* 65

PLATE IX

CHAMBORD, THE NORTH FAÇADE. The distant view of Chambord as one approaches it from the park is quite unforgettable. At the end of the long central avenue the château gradually fills the scene until at last the north façade appears in all its glory. In the centre is the 'keep', flanked by two massive towers and surmounted by the richly decorated upper storeys. The wings to right and left are of later date, and their style is more restrained. (Giraudon.) *facing p.* 70

PLATE X

BONAGUIL. The photograph is taken from the west side of the castle. The tall central building is the keep. Its northern (left-hand) portion dates from the thirteenth century. During the fifteenth century the southern portion (with machicolations) was added together with a tower housing the staircase. The curtain wall, which can be seen enclosing the keep, was fortified by Bringon de Roquefeuil (1482–1530). Three towers were added to the west side; the middle tower is square, the corner towers round. The massive tower at the north west (left-hand) corner is surmounted by 'Breton' machicolations in the form of stepped inverted pyramids (an archaeological curiosity which has aroused considerable discussion). Some time later Bringon de Roquefeuil enclosed the castle within a second curtain wall on which guns could be mounted. (Photothèque française.) *facing p.* 80

PLATE XI

JOSSELIN. Olivier de Clisson had the castle rebuilt when he became its owner in 1320. The view is of the façade overlooking the River Out, which was mainly Olivier de Clisson's work. But (like its contemporary the Bastille) the curtains at that time were much higher than they are today. The castle was dismantled in 1488 by order of François, duc de Bretagne. A few years later Jean, duc de Rohan, rebuilt the castle and turned it into a country seat, adding a pseudo-wall-walk, 'Breton' machicolations, and the tall, two-storey dormers above. (J. Roubier.) *facing p.* 81

PLATE XII

CARROUGES, THE GATE-HOUSE. Carrouges, near Alençon (Orne) is a large and rather incongruous structure made up of buildings dating from the fifteenth to the seventeenth centuries. Its most attractive feature is the gatehouse, which stands alone at some distance from the castle itself. On the dormer windows are the arms of Cardinal Jean le Veneur, Bishop of Lisieux from 1505 to 1543. The building is square and has a vast saddle-back roof and corner turrets. The masonry is of red brick embellished with black brick lozenges in the style of the Louis XII wing at Blois. The whole of the ornamentation – including the pediments over the dormers – is Flamboyant Gothic. Although dating from the reign of Louis XII it shows no indication whatever of Renaissance influence. (J. Roubier.) *facing p.* 84

PLATE XIII

BLOIS, COURTYARD FAÇADE OF THE FRANCIS I WING. The photograph clearly shows the contrast between the two parts of the façade. The great open staircase was added when the building was almost completed. (Roger Viollet.) *facing p.* 85

PLATE XIV

ECOUEN. This aerial photograph shows clearly the bastioned plan of the *fausse-braie*, which has survived intact on the south side of the building. The part of it on the north side was, however, demolished to make way for the great terrace just visible on the right of the photograph. The porch in the centre of the north wing (on the right) was a later addition by Jean Bullant. (Photothèque française.) *facing p.* 92

PLATE XV

FONTAINE-HENRI. The original castle was rebuilt by Jean d'Harcourt, its owner from 1496 to 1548. It comprises a main building and a large pavilion at right angles to it. Its special interest lies in the diversity of its styles. The right-hand part of the main building (including the square staircase tower) is a good example of the opulent Flamboyant style made fashionable by the redecoration of Amboise under Charles

VIII. On the two left-hand bays of the main building and on the adjoining façade (at right-angles to it) of the large pavilion the Gothic style has been replaced by Early French Renaissance in an almost exact copy of Gaillon. A further transition is noticeable on the tall dormer and on the west façade of the pavilion, which show a definite Classical trend. (J. Roubier.) *facing p.* 93

PLATE XVI
VALENÇAY. In its present form the château comprises two wings set at right angles. The north wing dates from the sixteenth and the west wing from the seventeenth and eighteenth centuries. The north wing (in the centre of the photograph) was almost certainly built by Jacques d'Etampes, who married in 1540 and died in 1575. The main structure of the west wing (just visible on the right) dates from the second quarter of the seventeenth century; but it underwent considerable alteration in 1770, when the second great tower was added at the south corner (J. Roubier.) *facing p.* 96

PLATE XVII
ANCY-LE-FRANC. The Courtyard. Ancy-le-Franc is the most outstanding example in France of the Italian School. The treatment of the façades on the courtyard is typical of the period. (J. Roubier.) *facing p.* 97

PLATE XVIII
CHENONCEAUX. The photograph shows the successive stages in the building of the castle. The 'Tour de Marques' (extreme left) is all that remains of the old feudal castle pulled down by Thomas Bohier when he built his new home on the piles of the former tannery in the Cher river. This new castle is seen with its four angle towers on the left of the photograph. When Diane de Poitiers came into possession of the property in the middle of the sixteenth century she built a bridge connecting the castle with the left bank of the river. Many years later, in 1580, Catherine de Médicis used the bridge to carry the three-storey galleries shown in the centre and on the right of the photograph. (Danèse-Rapho.) *facing p.* 104

PLATE XIX
JOINVILLE, LE GRAND JARDIN. Le Grand Jardin is a country mansion of moderate size, built by Claude de Guise in 1546, at the foot of the old castle of Joinville. The Classical style was then making its first appearance in France (notably at Saint Maur and Ancy-le-Franc). Le Grand Jardin seems to show that its owner was anxious to keep abreast of the times. (Boudot-Lamotte.) *facing p.* 112

PLATE XX
ANET, THE DOME OF THE CHAPEL. The chapel was one of the few buildings that survived the pillage of Anet by the Black Band. It is a small church on a symmetrical plan in the form of a Greek cross, with cupola, and is an exact copy of Italian churches of the period. Its appearance in France created a new style of religious architecture. Philibert Delorme was very proud of his interior decoration of the coffered dome with its interlacing curves and diminishing panels; he refers to it in his *Premier Tome de l'Architecture* (fol. 112). The pattern on the dome is reproduced in the paving of the chapel. (Boudot-Lamotte.) *facing p.* 113

PLATE XXVII
> TANLAY. The photograph shows the court of honour, the main building beyond (with twin pilasters framing the windows) and the two corner turrets surmounted by pointed domes. The courtyard has an open front and a rather unusual monumental extrance. (Paul Angoulvent.) *facing p.* 136

PLATE XXVIII
> MAISONS, THE ENTRANCE FAÇADE. Maisons, one of the earliest buildings in the French Classical style, is considered to be François Mansart's masterpiece. Although strictly conforming to the rules, the architect is obviously in search of movement and pictorial effect. (Rene-Jacques.) *facing p.* 142

PLATE XXIX
> LE CHAMP DE BATAILLE, CENTRAL PAVILION OF ONE OF THE WINGS. The masonry of this most unusual château is of brick and stone; but the massive pavilions forming the central motifs of the two large wings are built entirely in stone. M. Hautecoeur makes this comment: 'The pavilions, capped with *dômes à l'impériale*, the long balcony, the columns and openings, the varying proportions of brick and stone all seem like some rustic interpretation of the art of François le Vau.' (François le Vau's work had much in common with that of his elder brother, Louis). (Boudot-Lamotte.) *facing p.* 143

PLATE XXX
> DAMPIERRE, THE GARDEN FAÇADE. The dignified simplicity of this façade gives the impression that François Mansart was making a demonstration of the new style – even more noticeably than on the entrance side, which is built on a horseshoe plan. The only ornamentation is on the central frontispiece, which (like Maisons) is a doubly-projecting feature; but it has only two orders of columns and no upper storey dominating the façade. (J. Roubier.) *facing p.* 148

PLATE XXXI
> OMONVILLE. According to a report made by M. Lucien Prieur and preserved in the archives of the Office of Historical Monuments, Paris, Omonville was built in 1754 for the iron master, Robert-Philibert Le Carpentier, by Chartier, an architect from Conches (Eure). It is a good example of the restrained style of a Louis XV château, with its convex lintels embellished with brace-ornaments (except on the frontispiece of the ground floor, which have round-arched openings). In style, however, it lacks some of the refinement of contemporary châteaux built by Paris architects. The photograph shows the front façade, which is exactly similar to the façade on the garden side. The central portion of the façade – both on the front and on the garden – has an extra storey, which breaks the unity of the roof. (Boudot-Lamotte.) *facing p.* 149

PLATE XXXII
> FONTAINEBLEAU, COUR DE LA FONTAINE. The Fountain Courtyard, which overlooks the lake and is the most attractive part of the palace, dates, for the most part, from the sixteenth century. The large pavilion at the south-west corner (left of photograph) was, however, built by Ange-Jacques Gabriel in 1751. (J. Roubier-Rapho.) *facing p.* 156

over one of the doors. It is thought that Pablo Picasso has now decided to decorate other rooms with his own paintings. (Lapie-Photothèque française.) *facing p.* 177

PLATE XXXIX
VERSAILLES, THE FAÇADES OVERLOOKING THE GARDENS. These form part of the buildings erected by Le Vau around the old Louis XIII château. They were begun in 1668, but not completed until after Le Vau's death (on October 11th, 1670). The great west façade (centre of photograph) was originally more accentuated than it is today; the two upper floors were set back to allow space for a terrace over the ground floor. When Hardouin-Mansart built the Galerie des Glaces (1628–84) the terrace was suppressed and the façade assumed its present form. (E. Marton.) *facing p.* 182

PLANS

BOOK JACKET
VALS. Vals is deservedly famous, not only for its remarkable state of preservation but also because of its magnificent position overlooking the artificial lake created by the Bort dam. Over the door are the arms of the 'd'Estaing family (*de France au chef d'or*) who acquired the domain in 1422. But the castle must be of considerably earlier date. (Danèse-Rapho.)

| TRANSLATOR'S NOTE

Although the English word 'castle' is the exact linguistic equivalent of the French word 'château', it has acquired, over the years, a somewhat different meaning.

The French word 'château' is equally applicable to a Plantagenet fortress such as Gisors and to an elegant, seventeenth-century country mansion such as Dampierre. It is true that the word 'château-fort' specifically denotes a *fortified* castle; but the distinction is not often made.

The English word 'castle', however, in its current usage, generally implies an ancient, fortified castle of the type that became (militarily speaking) obsolete by the end of the fifteenth century.

In order to convey as accurately as possible to English readers this historical distinction between 'castle' and 'château', the former has been used only where the original text refers to a fortified castle. In all other cases the word 'château' has been used, as in the original text.

H.E.H.

FOREWORD |

A great number of works have already been published on the Châteaux of France.

It is impossible to mention more than a few of many excellent monographs available, as, for example, the collection of 'Petites Monographies', edited by Eugène Lefèvre-Pontalis and Marcel Aubert; or the scholarly works on *Le Château de Blois*, by the brothers Lesueur (1921), and on *Gaillon*, by Mlle. Chirol (1952).

Apart, however, from these detailed studies, other works of a more general character began to appear at a very early date. Du Cerceau, for instance, wrote, *Les plus excellents bastimens de France* between 1576 and 1579. The middle of the nineteenth century saw a steady increase in books on the subject, notably, *La Guienne Militaire*,[1] by Léo Drouyn (1865), *Palais, châteaux, hôtels et maisons de France* by Sauvageot (1867), and *Les châteaux historiques de la France* by d'Eyriès (1877–81). The twentieth century was also prolific in publications of this kind. Jean de Foville and Auguste Le Sourd were first in the field with *Les châteaux de France*, in 1912. Several other publishing houses followed quickly with a number of major productions, competing for what proved to be a popular demand: Messrs. Contet produced *Les anciens châteaux de France* (1913–33); Vincent Fréal published *Les châteaux et manoirs de France* (1934–39); Tel Publications followed with *Les Châteaux de France* by Ernest de Ganay (1948–53). Meanwhile, Henry Soulange-Bodin was producing a series of studies on the castles of Normandy (1928–29), of Maine and

---

[1] Guienne (or Guyenne) was the name given to part of the old province of Aquitaine after its conquest by King Phillip II of France.

Anjou (1934), Burgundy (1942), and Berry (1946). More recently M. Jacques-Mérillau published a book on the *Châteaux en Gironde* (1956) and M. François Enaud *Les châteaux forts en France* (1958). All these recent publications are fully illustrated, and the information they contain was collected for the most part from the actual owners of the castles concerned. All are valuable sources of reference. They are, nevertheless, only monographic studies of places treated in isolation; they make no attempt to co-ordinate their conclusions into a broad survey of the subject as a whole.

Those in search of works dealing with the wider issues involved are recommended to read, in the first place, d'Enlart's *Manuel* (2nd edition, published by Jean Verrier in 1932), which deals with the Middle Ages. It must be admitted, however, that the writer has involved himself in such detailed archeological research that it is extremely difficult to disentangle from it the main principles underlying the evolution of French fortified castles. Other more recent publications, however, are free of this fault and have followed a definitely historical plan in making their observations. Amongst them are *L'architecture militaire en Bretagne* by Roger Grand (*Bulletin monumental* 1951 and 1952), a work of wider scope than its title suggests and a useful source of general information; *Châteaux, donjons et places fortes* by M. Raymond Ritter (1953), written in a lively, polemical style (one of the author's main objects being to refute – as others have already done – the views put forward in 1898 by Marcel Dieulafoy in a treatise on the Château-Gaillard); and, finally, Mr. Sidney Toy's *A History of Fortification from 3000 B.C. to A.D. 1700* (London, 1955). The immense period of some fifty centuries covered by this last book has produced a mass of information enabling the author to put forward a number of extremely interesting suggestions.

The most important work on the modern period is *L'Histoire de l'architecture classique en France* by M. Louis Hautecoeur (1943–57). It would be wrong, however, to suppose that this masterly study has completely exhausted the subject so far as castles are concerned. Having made a broad survey of the development of French architecture as a whole the author finds himself forced to delve deeply into the study of the

B

Louvre and Versailles at the expense – if not at the risk of entirely neglecting – other monuments he considers of lesser importance. He is also inclined to give less and less attention to the study of castles as such because in the course of time they become increasingly indistinguishable from the great urban mansions, which, from the architectural point of view, are of more interest than those in rural districts.

Very few of the works mentioned (whether they be collections of monographs or educational publications) have covered the whole period – as Roger Grand and Sidney Toy have done – from the Middle Ages up to modern times. But these two writers were concerned with the purely military aspects of the subject, and they were therefore obliged to extend their studies over the whole relevant period. So far as we know, the only book which covers the whole period from earliest times up to the present day is M. Pierre du Colombier's *Le château de France*, published in 1960. This is a new and original work, but it might more correctly bear the title 'French castles and their owners', for it is essentially a study of the castle from the social point of view; the author studiously avoids any architectural comment, for the reason (as he says) that 'this has been done often enough already'.

It would seem, therefore, that although so much material has already been published, there would be some merit in an honest attempt to produce the first comprehensive, architectonic study covering the subject from its earliest beginnings to the present day.

The question at once arises as to the exact meaning of the word, 'château'. It is often used today to describe buildings which have – or seem to have – little in common, as, for example, a medieval fortress and a modern country house. It may be objected, therefore, that the subject comprises such widely dissimilar elements that an attempt at a comprehensive study would fail. We cannot accept this view. Whatever the period or style, every château has one fundamental characteristic; it is a place to be lived in; a residence. That is why the desire for comfort and even elegance becomes apparent at an early stage. In the keep at Chambois (Orne), for example, from the second half of the twelfth century

onwards the pillars of the fireplaces and the corbels supporting
the floors are very finely carved. As time went on the great
houses set an increasingly high standard of luxury, and
fortified castles during the reigns of Charles V and Charles
VI – the Louvre, Méhun-sur-Yèvre, Pierrefonds, etc. – were
furnished and decorated in the most sumptuous manner.
Once these castles had lost their military importance they
quickly became transformed into country seats of the type
we know today. But some time was to elapse before considerations of defence could be completely ignored. We shall see
later how, in the third quarter of the fifteenth century, Le
Plessis-Bourré introduced a new type of fortified castle that
was to serve as a model for the great Renaissance houses;
and it was by successive modifications of this plan that the
castle developed into the modern country seat.

There was a noticeable lack of uniformity, over the centuries, in the rate of growth of castle-building in France. The
feudal period was followed by a long pause during the reigns
of Saint Louis and his successors up to the Hundred Years'
War; it increased again under Charles V and Charles VI,
died down after Agincourt (1415) and again revived during
the second half of the fifteenth century, reaching its peak at
the Renaissance, during which the old medieval fortress
became transformed into the purely residential château of the
modern era. Both Francis I and Henry II realised that the
erection of magnificent private castles would add not only
beauty but also prestige to the royal domains; they therefore
encouraged their subjects to build. The letters patent raising
the barony of Montmorency into a dukedom in July 1551
mention (as one of the Constable's titles to the Royal favour)
that he had built at Chantilly and Ecouen 'two of the finest
and most excellently built houses in the whole Kingdom'.
Henry IV followed the same policy at the end of the wars of
religion. In his *Histoire du duc d'Epernon* (published in 1663,
II, 2) Guillaume Girard records that 'His Majesty urged the
greater part of the most wealthy members of the nobility to
plan the erection of fine houses', and points out that Cadillac
was built as a result of the King's personal intervention.
During the first half of the seventeenth century the 'back-
to-the-land' policy laid down by Henry IV and his minister,

Sully, was a powerful incentive to the building of castles by the rural aristocracy.

This development, however, was arrested by Louis XIV, whose ideas on the subject were strongly opposed to those of his predecessors. He was determined to uproot the aristocracy from their lands and to bring them under his personal control at Court. But castle-building revived after the King's death and continued throughout the eighteenth century until the Revolution. It was again resumed after the Restoration and it reached unprecedented levels during the Second Empire and the Third Republic. The end came, finally and irrevocably, in 1914.

The story of the building of the castles of France would be incomplete without some reference to those that were subsequently destroyed, not through war or civil disorders, but by deliberate and wholesale demolition in time of peace at two different periods of French history.

The first series of demolitions was the work of Richelieu. Fully aware of the political instability which had marked the beginning of the reign of Louis XIII, the Cardinal was determined to forestall any possible trouble from the somewhat turbulent nobility. Richelieu's policy in this matter was so ruthless that M. Pierre du Colombier, in his *Le château de France*, devotes a whole chapter to the subject under the title 'Richelieu, the enemy of the castle', that is to say, of the fortified castle. Not even the royal castles were spared; Pierrefonds was dismantled in 1622 on the pretext of excesses committed locally by its garrison; later, in 1652, Coucy shared the same fate (on Mazarin's orders) as a punishment for it's governor's support of the Fronde.[1] These ancient fortresses had by no means lost all their military value, for when Clément Métezean (the engineer who built the ramparts at La Rochelle) tried to blow up the keep at Coucy he succeeded only in destroying the interior vaulting and in producing cracks in the walls; the huge tower remained standing.[2]

[1] 'La Fronde' was the name given to the insurrection against Mazarin's rule during the minority of Louis XIV. It began in 1648 and ended finally in 1653.

[2] It will be remembered that it was destroyed by the Germans in 1917.

The demolitions carried out during the French Revolution
are perhaps better known to the general public than those of
Richelieu's time. It is true, as M. Pierre du Colombier points
out (p. 233), that 'far fewer castles were deliberately destroyed
by the Revolution than by Richelieu'. But the most serious
damage was done during the period between the Revolution
and the Restoration by the notorious Black Band, who were
able to buy up for a mere song (for subsequent demolition)
properties either confiscated by the State or so badly damaged
by looting that their owners could not afford to repair them.
A great number of famous castles were wholly or partially
destroyed in this way; and these were no longer mere ancient
keeps of mainly archaeological interest; they were master-
pieces of French architecture. Among them were Gaillon,
Anet, Chanteloup; and many others.

The Romantic period put a stop to these acts of vandalism.
The creation of the Commission of Historic Monuments on
December 29th, 1837, was evidence of official determination
to safeguard the artistic heritage of France. But the process
of classification was too slow to prevent a number of such
buildings falling into the hands of the speculator. In 1872 an
individual of the name of Verdolin stripped La Bâtie d'Urfé
of its interior decoration and of furniture that had been
preserved almost intact since the Renaissance. On April 30th,
1881, the whole of the sculptured fragments from Montal,
(dormer windows, medallions, friezes, etc.), were allowed to
be put up for auction. Again, in 1902, the ruins of Grignan
were purchased, broken up, and the sculptures sold by auction – the purchaser being a descendant of the family who
built the château!

We may end, however, on a more cheerful note. In 1909,
after the destruction of the interior decoration of La Bâtie
d'Urfé, the house itself was on the point of being dismantled
and transported stone by stone across the Atlantic, when it
was rescued by the learned society, 'Diana', of Montbrison,
and purchased outright. Montal had similar good fortune.
Maurice Fenaille acquired the ruins and eventually succeeded, after tremendous efforts, in collecting together almost
all the fragments that had been stripped off it by the house-
breakers, and completely restored the building. Raymond

Poincaré, then President of France, honoured the place by an official visit in August 1913.

No one builds castles nowadays – a fact (one might suggest), that gives even greater value to these historic monuments. But a new and powerful safeguard is at work. The development of the tourist trade, with its coach trips, its floodlighting, its 'son et lumière', has aroused public interest in historic castles and become a significant source of income to their owners, who have now formed their own professional association, 'La Demeure Historique'.

Without being unduly optimistic, one may be reasonably certain that the deplorable vandalism of which such castles as La Bâtie d'Urfé, Montal and Grignan were victims will never be repeated.

1 *Angers, The Field Gate*

CHAPTER ONE

| THE MIDDLE AGES

In the etymological sense, a castle (*castellum*) is essentially a
fortified place. Its basic feature, the *motte*, or mound, also
known as the 'keep' (*dunio*), is thought to date from the time
of the Norman invasions, that is to say, from the very early
years of the tenth century. The mound, or small, man-made
hill, was enclosed by a rampart thrown up around it, usually
surmounted by a palisade or hedge. Set up a tower on the
mound – and you have a castle.

Up to the end of the eleventh century, the tower (or 'keep',
as we shall now call it), was built of wood; but the rampart or
wall surrounding it was of earth, and remained so until a
much later date.

Our knowledge of these wooden forts comes from ancient
records and also from the Bayeux Tapestry, which leading
historians now believe to date from the last quarter of the
eleventh century. If we compare the rough drawing of Dinan
(Côtes-du-Nord), as shown on the Tapestry, with the descrip-
tions of the Castle of Merkem (near Dixmude, Belgium) and
other fortified places in that area, as given in the life of Jean
de Commines, Bishop of Thérouanne,[1] we shall find that the
types are identical, although these places are miles apart.
Each has its mound, surrounded by a trench and crowned
by a sturdy palisade. Within the palisade, in the middle of the

[1] See Bibliography, Mortet (Victor), *Recueil*, I, pp. 313–315.

mound, is a redoubt which dominates the whole. The fort itself is reached by a footbridge crossing the trench. It is worth noting that the Tapestry shows soldiers with lighted torches setting fire to the fort – a clear indication that it is made of wood.

We find, therefore, in these timber structures, all the essential features of the Norman fortified castle: the mound, the keep (or central redoubt), and the surrounding 'chemise', or palisade.

1 | The Norman Keeps

The replacement of wood by stone in the construction of these castles was an unhurried process. The Bayeux Tapestry shows that at the end of the eleventh century stone fortresses were still very rare. Of the five fortified castles shown on the Tapestry only one is of stone – and it is not easy to identify; all the others are of wood.

The use of stone became more common during the twelfth century. The castle of Ardres (Pas-de-Calais), built presumably in the early years of the century by Arnoul, the lord of the manor, is given a flattering description in the chronicles of Lambert d'Ardres;[1] but it was, nevertheless, a wooden structure. The less-important keep at Longueil (Seine-Maritime), dating from about 1125, and carefully studied by R. Quenedey[2] before it was destroyed, was, however, already built in stone.

In castles built for kings and other princely rulers, the stone keep, however, had already made its appearance more than a century earlier.

The oldest example still in existence is the castle of Langeais. According to his grandson, Fulk le Réchin, and to a number of local records, it was founded by the Count of Anjou, Fulk Nerra (977–1040). It must already have been standing in 966, for a charter granted by Odo, first Count

---

[1] See Victor Mortet, Bibliography, "Recueil" I, pp. 183–185.
[2] *Bulletin Monumental*, 1931.

of Blois, bears the date of the siege of Langeais (*ad obsidionem castelli Langiacensis*), February 12th, 966.[1]

The keep is rectangular, its inside measurements being 53 feet by 23 feet. The north and east walls are still standing, up to a height of about forty feet. Its quadrilateral form, typical of timber-built keeps, shows its direct derivation from the earlier, wooden type; so also does the absence of any stone staircase or of vaulting on the upper floors. Although built at the end of the tenth century, the masonry is almost exactly in the Gallo-Roman tradition; the walls, 3 feet 9 inches thick on the north side and 4 feet 9 inches on the east, are made of stone rubble packed together with mortar and surfaced with roughly-squared small stone (*opus constructum lapillis*). The bays have the semicircular Norman arch, with keystones of alternate stone and brick. At each corner, and in the middle of the east façade, the walls are supported by buttresses of medium height, probably added at some later date to strengthen the building, which was besieged on several occasions.

All that remains today is the ground level and the first floor; but it is likely that the original building had a second floor. Following the tradition in all Norman keeps, the ground floor has no direct communication with the exterior. (The door visible on the north side is the result of some later modification.) The ground floor could only be reached by a ladder or wooden stairway from the first floor. In 1930 Adrien Blanchet discovered, in the middle of the ground floor, the foundations of a pillar which helped to support the floor above. Six bays are cut in the walls of the first floor, most of them being windows. The last bay on the left of the east façade is the entrance to the castle: it was always the practice, in Norman keeps, to site the entrance high above the ground, out of reach of unwelcome visitors.

The toothing stones of two walls set at right angles to the façade are clearly visible round this door. These walls formed part of an adjoining, smaller tower, usually known as the

---

[1] See Lot: *Etudes sur le règne de Hugues Capet*, pp. 178, n.2, and 423–36. The original of the charter is in the archives of the Indre-et-Loire Department, but one of the figures of the date is torn, and two inaccuracies have been noted: the number of the indiction (which appears to have been written over an erasure), and the year of the reign of Hugh Capet. We agree with Lot's reading on this point.

'small keep', which was, in fact, an enclosed staircase. We shall give some further explanations on this point when dealing with the castle of Loches.

Summing up, Langeais may be described as being novel in conception, but the methods used in its construction are still those of the Late Empire.

Another stone keep at Montbazon – also in Touraine – must be more or less contemporary with Langeais. Fulk Nerra records it as being under construction in the Charter No. 31 of the cartulary of Cormery, granted by Robert le Pieux[1] at the request of Abbé Thibault (977–1066). It forms part of the strategic plan which includes Langeais and cover: Tours by commanding the valleys that converge on the citys the Loire at Langeais, the Indre at Montbazon and the Cher at Montrichard (rebuilt in the twelfth century).

Montbazon was often besieged. (Gatian de Clérambault records six sieges between 944 and 1117). As a result, so much rebuilding and restoration have taken place that considerable caution is advised in making a study of it. It is clear, however, that originally it had much in common with Langeais; the same rectangular plan; approximately the same interior dimensions (51 feet by 31 feet). The walls, too, are of the same type, faced with small stone, but thicker (8 feet on the north and east). The door is placed high up on the northern side, 26 feet above the ground. There is the same absence of vaulting and of any stone staircase; each floor was ceiled, and communication between them was by ladder only.

As it stands today, the building is 93 feet high and has three floors above the ground floor. The absence of buttresses on the west and south sides justifies the assumption that there was none on the original building. The east and north sides are supported by six buttresses, of which two are rectangular and flat, like those at Langeais; the other four are semicylindrical, and have the advantage of giving a clearer field of fire to the defenders. These semicylindrical buttresses were almost certainly added later to the original structure; but the thickness of the joints shows that these buttresses are of very early date.

[1] King Robert II (996–1031).

The west side of the castle is flanked by a rectangular 'small keep' (now in a very ruinous condition), which was probably a covered staircase similar to that at Langeais. The irregular small stone facing of its walls shows that it belongs to the same period as the oldest parts of the main tower; but it must have been an addition to the original building since the original entrance to the keep appears to have been on the north side.

The castle of Loches, which lies to the south of Montbazon and Montrichard and (strategically) covers them both, belonged from the ninth century onwards to the Counts of Anjou. It almost certainly formed part of the strategic plan drawn up by Fulk Nerra against Tours. As a matter of fact, no record exists to show that it was he who rebuilt the castle. Its general appearance suggests that it is of a period considerably later than that of Langeais; and M. Jean Valléry-Radot put forward the very plausible suggestion that it was built at the end of the eleventh century. (See Plate II.)

But a difficulty arose later. After examining the building closely, M. Valléry-Radot noticed that considerable restoration and repair had been done to the west side. Here, for about fifty feet, or half-way up from the ground, the external façade is definitely of earlier date than the rest; the wall, however, has at some later date been doubled in thickness and its height raised to the top of the building. Further, this western façade, unlike the others, had originally no buttresses; those which now support it at the angles were obviously built on later. It is clear, therefore, that the walls of the original keep had only half the strength of the present ones, and had no buttresses – which, in fact, seems to have been the position both at Langeais and Montbazon. As Fulk Nerra died in 1040, it is surely reasonable to conclude – as M. Valléry-Radot is inclined to do – that he was nearing the end of his life when he began the reconstruction of Loches, and that he died before the scheme was completed. If this be so, the work must have been resumed on a larger scale some time later, with the result we see today.

This magnificent, rectangular mass of masonry has a height of 123 feet; its interior measurements are 66 feet by 26 feet; the walls are 9 feet thick. As is often the case, it stands, not in the centre, but on the edge (and, in fact, on the weaker side) of the enclosure which surrounds the vast 'bailey' or lower court, covering the whole upper level of the mound. The walls are revetted in medium (instead of small) stone. The thickness of the joints, however – a little over an inch – betrays a certain lack of finish in the masonry. Like those of Montbazon, the buttresses, which were part of the original structure (except, as we have seen, on the west façade), are semicylindrical. The 'small keep', erected on the less exposed north side, is sufficiently well preserved to allow one to visualise its original plan. The entrance is 10 feet above the present ground level. Stairs, built on to the inside of the walls, led up to the door of the main building at a considerably higher level on the first floor. As the staircases were entirely unprotected, the defenders could easily deny their use to any attacker who might have gained entrance. The chapel was on the third floor; its semi-domed apse is still visible. The keep itself had three floors above the ground floor. The latter, used as a storeroom, was, like most others of its kind, completely unlit except for the few loopholes necessary for ventilation. The upper floors were lit by a few narrow bays with semicircular arches; it is still possible to trace the remains of three fireplaces built on to one of the walls.

The ground floor is divided in two by a wall which gives support to the beams carrying the floor above. A similar construction, it will be remembered, is to be seen at Langeais, where a central pillar replaced the dividing wall.

On the other hand, a novel feature, which contrasts both with Langeais and with Montbazon, is the way in which the stone staircases are built on to the interior sides of the walls. The siting of these staircases is indicative, also, of the cunning displayed in all Norman keeps with the object of baffling any of the enemy who may have succeeded in gaining entry to the fortress. There is no direct communication between one flight of stairs and the one immediately above. From the first to the second floor the stairs come out in the south-east corner; from the second to the third, in the north-west corner. Coming up, therefore, from the second floor, one would have to cross the room to go up to the floor above.

The castle of Beaugency (Loiret) differs from those we have

just been studying in that it lies virtually outside the Angevin area. It was a frontier post between the royal domain and the County of Blois. Its massive size and many other features suggest that it was contemporary with Loches. Its plan is rectangular; the masonry is of rough, medium-sized stone (except in the buttresses, where the stone is more carefully graded). The original bays are narrow; the interior measurements are 54 feet by 41 feet; the north wall is 12¼ feet thick at the base and 8 feet thick at the upper floors.

The mound on which it was built was levelled in the nineteenth century, and the bases of the walls uncovered. They were found to consist of gigantic blocks of stone, after the fashion of the Gallo-Roman curtain-walls, of which the foundations were often made from great stones taken from ancient buildings. Amongst some of these blocks Adrien Blanchet even claims to have identified two fragments of Roman milestones.

The general features of the building are similar to those we have already met elsewhere. The buttresses are flat; the ground floor has no communication with the exterior and is lit only by loopholes; there is no vaulting on the upper floors; the entrance is on the first floor. Finally, in order to baffle the enemy, the staircase leading down to the lower room ends at a point 20 feet above ground level.

Beaugency differs, nevertheless, from the castles we have so far examined by the fact that it has no 'small keep'. The only means of entry was by a movable bridge between the door and the top of the curtain wall. Although the latter has now disappeared, an engraving by Claude Chastillon shows that it was still in existence in the seventeenth century. The central keep is depicted, surrounded by double curtain-walls. The ground floor, too, had double barrel-vaulting supported in the middle, not by a dividing wall but by a row of three arches. Many years later, probably in the fifteenth century, similar arcades were added at each storey to support the floors above.

It is almost certain that in Normandy, the richest domain in France, stone castles appeared at a very early date. Up to 1883 a keep still existed at Avranches (that is to say, on the borders of Brittany), in which the herring-bone masonry (*opus spicatum*) interspersed with courses of brick and the brick voussoirs of the windows suggest very ancient construction, almost contemporary with that of Langeais. Owing, no doubt, to extensive restoration and rebuilding Normandy, however, can no longer lay claim to any castle of earlier date than the twelfth century (except Gisors).

The great builder of fortified castles was, of course, the English king, Henry I Beauclerc, who had become duke of Normandy in 1106. In 1119, Louis VI, the quarrelsome monarch who had acceded to the throne of France in 1108, took upon himself to make a rather foolhardy expedition deep into Henry's territory, the 'Vexin Normand',[1] where, for his pains, he was crushingly defeated at Brémule. Such an attack from his turbulent neighbour could not fail to put the English king on his guard. In 1123, the chronicler Robert de Torigni (alias Robert du Mont) gives a list of eleven castles built or strengthened by Henry I and covering the whole Normandy frontier to a depth of twenty or twenty-five miles. Judging by those that have survived at Arques, Falaise, Domfront and Vire, these keeps were nearly all of the rectangular type.

Let us look at Falaise (Calvados), which is in a better state of preservation than the others, and was carefully restored by Ruprich-Robert in 1864. It replaced an older castle famous in popular lore by being thought to have sheltered the loves of Robert le Diable, duke of Normandy, and Arlette, the pretty laundrymaid, who were the parents of William the Conquerer. (See Plate III.)

The interior measurements of the present keep are impressive: 65 feet by 55 ft. It was of relatively late date, as witness the well-cut ashlar, the string-course ornamenting the building at the base of the second floor, and the twin bays of the same floor, which have carved capitals on the centre pillars. But, so far as the style of building is concerned, there is no feature that is not already familiar. The buttresses are flat, but have double offsets; the ground floor has a dividing wall and no means of communication with the exterior; there is a complete absence of vaulting; the staircase is built in the

---

[1] The Vexin, one of the old French Provinces, was divided into 'Norman' and 'French' Vexin.

thickness of the wall; the entrance is placed high up on the most sheltered (east) side of the first floor; and the chapel is in a projection built out from the first floor. A squat 'little keep' was added later on the far side, against the west façade. Its position is surprising, for this is the most exposed side of the building. But this tower carries no internal staircase; it is placed there for military reasons to cover a rocky platform against occupation by possible attackers.

A special feature should be noted. The rectangular keeps in the Loire valley have quoins of solid masonry, with buttresses applied on each face. At Falaise, however, the two corner buttresses are joined together, leaving a hollow space between them and the angle of the keep. This space is used either to house a spiral staircase or to be converted into small rooms, one of which has, quite understandably, been given the name of Arlette's Chamber. So far, therefore, as the interior arrangement is concerned, Falaise may be described as a keep having square turrets flanking each corner; but it should be added that these turrets project only very slightly from the main building and are in no way to be considered as having military use in outflanking possible attackers.

Rectangular buttress-turrets of a similar type were in common use in England on keeps built by the Normans at the end of the eleventh century. They are to be seen on the west side of the White Tower in London, on the keep of Rochester Castle, Kent, on the north side of Colchester Castle in Essex and at Castle Rising in Norfolk. The chapel also is built out at a corner of the first floor at Falaise, as it is at the Tower of London and at Colchester. Falaise, in fact, is of particular interest because its points of resemblance to the English castles allow one to define the typical features of a Norman keep of the period.

The Norman style died hard. Up to the second half (or even the last third) of the twelfth century it can still be found, for example, at Chambois (Orne), which is obviously of much later date, as witness the slightly battered bases of the walls (now buried) and the clawed bases and foliated capitals of the pillars supporting the hoods over the fireplaces. M. Xavier Rousseau suggests that it was built by William de Mandeville, who died in 1189, and who was one of the favourites of Henry II Plantagenet. The upper part of the building, however, with its machicolated battlements, was added in 1400.

Chambois is a rectangular keep of almost the same dimensions as those of Montbazon; its interior measurements are 51 feet by 31 feet and its height 86 feet. But the thickness of the walls (10 feet) is rather greater than is usual in eleventh-century castles. It has the customary Norman features: the ground floor has no communication with the exterior, and is lit only by loopholes; there is no vaulting, and the entrance is at the level of the first floor. It has, in addition, a peculiarity in common with Falaise and the English keeps: it is supported at the four corners by buttress-turrets projecting slightly beyond the walls but having no military value so far as flanking fire is concerned.

The disposition of the 'small keep', built on to the east face, should, however, be carefully noted. It will be remembered that at Loches the entrance to this extra tower was at a rather low level, and that the tower itself carried a staircase leading to the entrance to the main building, which was much higher up. The arrangement at Chambois, however, is entirely different. The ground floor of the small keep has no communication with the outside; access to it was by a trapdoor in the vault above. The entrance to the castle was made at the level of the first floor, and it leads to a well-lit room, serving as vestibule to the door of the main keep, which is on the same level. This arrangement is copied from the English castles of Rochester and Castle Rising, where the vestibule, or entrance-hall, as at Chambois, is well lit by several windows, and must have been a particularly pleasant room. (See p. 106.)

It is impossible to know whether similar dispositions existed at Falaise, because we have no details regarding the small keep (assuming that one existed there) that stood guard over the entrance to the castle. At the wooden castle of Ardres (Pas de Calais), however, and according to the description given by Lambert d'Ardres (see *Recueil*, I, pp. 183–85), it would seem that a similar arrangement existed, and that, amongst a maze of stairs and passages, there were some that led from the main building to a room he calls a 'loge' (or parlour) and from the 'loge' to the chapel (*item a domo in*

11 *The Keep, Loches*

logium . . . , *item de logio in oratorium sive capellam*). Lambert goes on to say that the chapel was situated in the upper part of the building, and to describe the 'loge' as a pleasant place where people would meet and converse. This 'loge', which was outside the main building, seems to correspond with the vestibule, or entrance-hall in the English castles. The chapel, no doubt, was on the floor above, over the vestibule, just as it is at Rochester. Lambert's account is particularly interesting because the fact that these rooms were intended for rest or recreation explains why, at Rochester, Castle Rising and Chambois, they have large windows opening on to the outside world – a somewhat risky innovation from the military point of view, which elicited some surprised comment from M. Paul Deschamps (vide *Congrès archéologique*, 1953, p. 298).

All the stone keeps we have been discussing developed from the original wooden towers and, like them, are quadrilateral in plan. But once the use of stone had become well established builders could turn their attention to other types. We find, for example, the Gallo-Roman type of rounded tower with flattened neck along the curtains (as at Senlis), or almost circular at the corners of the rampart as at the Archbishop's Palace (now the museum) at Tours. We think, too, that the Gallo-Roman fort was used as a model for the circular keeps found in certain castles. The oldest of these still standing is undoubtedly at Fréteval (Loir-et-Cher), and dates, most probably, from the middle of the eleventh century. The same type is found, not far from Fréteval, at Château-Renault (Indre-et-Loire) – dating from the end of the eleventh century – and also in the Norman Vexin at Neaufles and at Château-sur-Epte (Eure). Although it never became common, it was frequently used during the twelfth century.

It will be noted that these circular keeps, although in their general features they still conformed to the older rectangular types, differed from them (and followed the Gallo-Roman model) by having no buttress.

Whether rectangular or circular, however, all the keeps we have studied so far have the same essential features, which remained unchanged for more than a hundred years; that is to say, there was no communication between the ground floor and the exterior; the entrance was high above ground level; the floors were ceiled, not vaulted; and the window-openings were narrow, semicircular, and limited to the upper floors.

It was in masonry, however, that real progress was made. From the point of view of refinement, there is no comparison between Langeais and Falaise. Even the structure of the building itself – its walls and foundations – was improved. Judging by Langeais, Montbazon and Loches, the walls of rectangular keeps were originally quite bare. It was as a result of successive attacks that it was found necessary to support them with buttresses. At Langeais and Montbazon, for example, these were added to existing structures; at others, such as Beaugency, Loches and Falaise, the buttresses were incorporated in the original buildings. There was a tendency too, for walls to be made thicker. In earlier keeps – at Langeais, for example, and the west façade of Loches – the thickness was 4 feet 6 inches. This increases to 8 feet at Montbazon, Beaugency, and Château-sur-Epte, to over 9 feet at Loches and Neaufles, 10 feet at Château-Renault, and 10 feet 8 inches at Falaise. For similar reasons, wooden ladders and stairways were gradually replaced by stone staircases built on to the insides of walls; and the art of baffling a potential enemy was developed by cutting off any direct and continuous communication by stairway between the floors.

In contrast to the progress made in masonry, there seems to have been no advance in military ideas (so far as our present knowledge goes) during the eleventh century. It has often been observed that the art of defence, in regard to fortified places, was concerned only with the height or the thickness of the walls. No attempt was made to provide flanking fire; no projecting structure was conceived that could bring fire to bear on any attackers who had reached the foot of the walls. From this point of view, the rectangular fort was of the worst shape possible, because at each corner there was always an area completely uncovered by any defensive fire; which therefore allowed the enemy to slip through to the foot of the walls and undermine the building. This fault was remedied later, in theory at least, by the introduction of circular keeps; but it is in no way certain that those who first built them realised their superiority from the military point of view; they had been content merely to copy the plan of the Gallo-Roman tower.

The arrangements for defence were all located in the upper part of the building. The loopholes one finds on the ground floor of several keeps (Loches, Beaugency, Chambois, etc.) are not intended for archers' use; they are simply narrow slits cut in the wall to provide light and ventilation.

The crowning has disappeared from all existing Norman keeps; only by conjecture, therefore, is it possible to arrive at any conclusions as to the methods used in their defence.

There is good reason to suppose that the tops of the walls were crenellated. There is still, in fact, some evidence of eleventh-century crenellation at Chinon – not on a tower, but on the west curtain of the Château du Coudray,[1] which had been increased in height on three separate occasions. One can clearly see, on the outer face of the curtain, the outline of the battlements of the two earlier walls, the lower of which probably dates either from the count of Anjou, Geoffrey Martel, who became the lord of Chinon in 1044, or even perhaps from his predecessor, the count of Blois.

The existence of hoards on eleventh-century keeps has often been debated. These wooden galleries, built out from the exterior walls of the fort, had their floors pierced with holes through which various projectiles could be dropped upon any attackers who had reached the foot of the walls. They seem to have been unknown to the ancient world,[2] although Philo of Byzantium (III, 5) mentions a similar device which consisted of mobile parapets attached to the insides of the walls. These *coursières*, or runways, were known in France from the end of the eleventh century onwards; Adolphe de Dion (*Bulletin monumental*, 1867, p. 363) reports one on the curtain wall of the keep at Château-sur-Epte.

As to the hoards themselves, one certainly existed on the curtain of the west façade at Chinon; which leads us to suppose (if the date suggested is correct), that this form of defence was already known at the middle of the eleventh

---

[1] Chinon comprises *three* castles: Château Saint-Georges, Château du Milieu and Château du Coudray.
[2] We cannot agree with Viollet-le-Duc (see Bibliography) when he claims that hoards correspond to the galleries connecting wooden towers, referred to by Caesar in his *Commentaries* (VIII, 9).

century. It was used, in any case, in the first quarter of the twelfth century, as it is to be seen on several castles of that period: the keep at Huriel (Allier) – which, in M. Paul Deschamps' view, is contemporary with Loches and Beaugency (*Congrès archéologique*, 1938, p. 57); the keep at Loudun (Vienne), where the pointed arch over the door is evidence of a relatively late date; at Gisors, between the Governor's Gate and the Prisoner's Tower, dating from 1123, and at Carcassonne, which is more or less of the same period. The joists that carried the planking of the hoards were either supported on small trusses projecting from the walls (as at Gisors and, later, at Chambois), or they were inserted into slots or holes in the walls (as at Huriel, Loudun and Carcassonne); and it is by these rows of trusses or holes that the original existence of hoards is revealed.[1]

It was an essential feature of the defence of any keep to site the entrance high above the ground level. In certain cases – notably at Beaugency, Huriel and Châtillon-sur-Indre – the only means of access to the entrance was by a footbridge from the top of the 'chemise' (or curtain wall) of the castle. If a staircase was used for this purpose it was always enclosed in a 'small keep', as at Loches. At Château-sur-Epte, however, one finds a slightly different arrangement: the entrance to the courtyard surrounding the keep is through a small tower which has a door 13 feet above the ground; from this door an open staircase runs along the outer wall to the main entrance of the keep.

The most usual method of closing the entrance was by a plain wooden beam, which held the doors shut. When not in use, the beam was stowed away in a hole in the wall; such holes can still be seen in many keeps (at Montbazon, Loudun, Montrichard, Chambois, etc.).

Some speculation exists as to whether the footbridge leading to the entrance could be raised like a drawbridge. The pulley type of drawbridge was certainly known to the ancient world. The *sambuca* described by Vegetius (IV, 21)

---

[1] At Huriel and Carcassonne there are two rows of holes. The upper row carried the joists; the lower one carried a series of beams projecting slightly beyond the joists and fitted with oblique supports holding up the joists above. A drawing by Viollet-le-Duc (Vo 'hourd', Fig. 1) explains this arrangement very clearly. Later examples show only one row of holes.

was an instrument of this kind, and was used by the troops attacking a fortified place to pass from their mobile wooden siege-towers on to the top of the walls of the fort. But, so far as we know, there is no reason to believe that drawbridges existed in castles of the eleventh century. The brackets still to be seen in front of the entrance to the keep at Beaugency have neither the notches nor grooves necessary to house the swivel-pins of a drawbridge; they appear to have been nothing more than the supports for a footbridge.

It may be useful to complete this general survey by some remarks upon the interior dispositions of the eleventh-century castle. The chronicles left by Lambert d'Ardres give us some valuable information on this subject. We learn, for instance, that at the wooden castle of Ardres the ground floor was used as a store-room, that the apartment on the first floor was reserved for the master of the house, and that the kitchens were in a separate building. The same arrangement is also to be found in the stone-built castles. The ground floor is always cut off from any communication with the exterior, and is used as a store. Note also that originally the ground floor had no vaulting, and that a dividing wall was sometimes used to support the floor of the room above. From about 1100 onwards, however, we find vaulting in these ground-floor rooms at Beaugency (Loiret), Courcelles-les-Gisors (Oise) and at La Roche-Posay (Vienne). The room on the first floor is set aside for the master of the house. It is, in fact, the forerunner of the great hall, the main feature of all castles in the Middle Ages; and one soon sees efforts being made to give an air of comfort and even of elegance to this room. At Chambois, for instance, the corbels supporting the ties of the beams in the ceiling are decorated with ornamental carving. As to the kitchens of the eleventh century, the only traces still surviving, so far as we know, are at Gisors, and (as at Ardres) they are located outside the keep.

The details given by Lambert d'Ardres regarding the interior distribution of these castles were confirmed in 1927 by the excavation, up to a height of $6\frac{1}{2}$ feet, of the walls of the castle of Longueil (Seine-Maritime). These remains were sufficiently intact to allow one to follow, on the ground, the plan of the whole building. Most unfortunately, the walls themselves have since been destroyed, but a permanent record of them was made in a detailed description by R. Quenedey in the *Bulletin monumental*, 1931. Longueil, which dates probably from about 1125, was of only secondary importance. The wall surrounding the castle was merely an earth entrenchment; the internal dimensions of the keep were but 44 feet by 26 feet. But its general features are in every way similar to those of the great castles of the period, and indeed they give it a definitely Norman character. The keep was rectangular; it was buttressed, and the interior was divided by a party wall. The ground floor had no communication with the exterior, and the entrance was on the first floor. Two walls built out at right angles from the south-west corner indicate that a 'small keep' had once stood there, but it was impossible to determine whether it was used merely as an interior staircase (as at Loches) or as a vestibule (or 'loge') as at Ardres and Chambois. Unlike Falaise and Chambois, the corner buttresses were not joined together; but a winding staircase had been built in the thickness of the masonry at the north-west corner as at Falaise and at many of the English castles, such as the Tower of London, Rochester, Colchester, etc. The Norman character of the keep is confirmed by the position of the chapel, which is built on to the south wall, the apse projecting eastwards; a disposition which is also found at the Tower of London and at Colchester. Finally, adjoining the main building were a number of minor structures including the kitchen, which – as at Ardres – was located outside the keep itself.

2 | The Twelfth Century
The Plantagenet Castles

All archaeologists agree that the Crusades gave a valuable stimulus to the military leaders of the West. The Arab and Byzantine peoples had preserved their ancient traditions and were more advanced than the Crusaders in the art of military engineering.

During the twelfth century the Western commanders began seriously to study ancient treatises on the art of war, a subject which (it appeared) they had hitherto greatly neglected. Jean de Marmoutier records in his *Historia Ganfridi ducis Normannorum* that during the siege of Montreuil-Bellay in 1151, Geoffrey Plantagenet was engaged in reading Vegetius when a delegation arrived from the monks of Marmoutiers. Anxious to show them the fruit of his studies, he invited them to be present at the launching of an incendiary projectile based on the *falarique* described by Vegetius (IV, 8). Geoffrey Plantagenet, however, was only one of many others of his time who were seeking to improve their military knowledge. As a result, the art of defence began at last to emerge from centuries of stagnation and neglect. We find ample evidence, during this period, of repeated efforts to improve the design of the keep so as to permit flanking fire along the walls. But it must be admitted that these efforts were more often distinguished by their good intentions than by their efficacy.

Houdan (Seine-et-Oise) was built during the first thirty years of the twelfth century by Amaury de Montfort (1105–37). The builder was evidently aware of the rule laid down by Vitruvius (1. 5) to the effect that the keep should be circular or polygonal; he had also learned from Vegetius (IV, 2) the importance of bringing flanking fire to bear from the towers on to the walls. With the best of intentions he built a circular keep, flanked by four turrets, but he failed to perceive that the convex curve of the walls prevented the cross fire from the turrets from converging to cover the area between them. This disadvantage was accentuated by the fact that the turrets were solid throughout almost their entire height, thereby reducing even further their value for flanking purposes. The entrance, which was in one of the turrets, was 18 feet above ground level and considerably lower than the first floor; it opened on to a stairway of twenty steps cut in the thickness of the wall and leading straight up to the first floor.[1] This plan was ingenious and unquestionably superior to those we have met hitherto, where the entrance opened directly on to the main room of the keep.

The keep at Provins, erected by the Counts of Champagne

[1] We are indebted for these details to Adolphe de Dion (*Bulletin monumental*, 1905). The keep has now been turned into a water-tower, and therefore the interior can no longer be visited.

towards the middle of the twelfth century, shows evidence of the same intention and suffers from the same fault as that of Houdan. It is of octagonal design and is flanked by round turrets on four of its faces; but the turrets protrude so little that the whole external plan of the building could be contained in a perfect square, with the result that it is impossible to bring flanking fire to bear on the four walls that have no turrets.

The royal keep at Etampes, known as the 'Guinette Tower', is almost certainly of the same period (middle of the twelfth century) as those of Houdan and Provins; but it is in every way superior to either. From the design of three surviving capitals on the walls of the upper room, Eugène Lefevre-Pontalis (*Congrès, archéologique*, 1919, p. 40) suggests that it was built during the first quarter of the century. The keep has a very original four-leaved plan with four round towers mutually intersecting and providing excellent flanking cover between them. As at Houdan the entrance is placed midway between the ground level and the first floor; it opens on to a rib-vaulted passage passing through a wall 12 feet thick, and ends in a sheer drop of 12 feet above the floor of the lower room. From right and left of this passage two staircases built in the thickness of the wall lead respectively up to the first floor and down to the ground level.

The keep at Ambleny (Aisne), although, like Etampes, it has four massive towers, is on a slightly different plan. Instead of overlapping each other the towers are separated by very short curtains varying in length from 6 to 10 feet. It is less powerfully built than the keep at Etampes and is almost certainly of later date – probably towards the end of the twelfth century.

It is surprising, in view of the complexity of these plans and the considerable ingenuity shown in their elaboration, to find that the simpler and more effective rectangular design with four corner towers was so rarely used. It is found, however, in the royal castle at Niort, which dates apparently from the third quarter of the twelfth century and to which we shall return later; also in a number of keeps in the Poitou area; at Pouzauges and at Tiffauges (Vendée), and others. A striking characteristic common to these castles is that the keeps are four-sided and are strengthened at the corners by

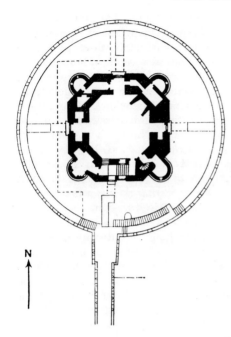

FIG. I.

PROVINS. *Plan of the keep, showing the inner wind enclosed by the original chemise.*

N

THE KEEP AT ETAMPES

The plan shows the section of the keep at a point half-way between ground level and the first floor.

Note the arrangement of the entrance.

N

solid square turrets with rounded corners. The same principle is followed in the Gouzon keep at Chauvigny (Vienne). This was originally of the rectangular, eleventh-century type (exemplified by Beaugency), but as a result of later modification its width was doubled and solid corner turrets were added. It is very difficult to determine the date of these three keeps at Pouzauges, Tiffauges, and Chauvigny. At Pouzauges all the floors have barrel vaulting similar to that of the two lower floors of the south tower at Niort; all the buttresses supporting the curtains are semicircular, as they also are at Niort. We are therefore led to assume that Pouzauges, Tiffauges and Chauvigny are of the same period as the great neighbouring castle of Niort, and that they can therefore be dated from the second half of the twelfth century.

Leaving the Poitou country we come now to Paris and to the great tower of the Temple, long since disappeared. This also was a square keep with round turrets at each corner. There is ample evidence that it is of later date than that of Niort; the walls have battered bases; the rooms on each of the four floors have pointed vaulting, the ribs of the four panels being supported on a central pillar. It was most probably built in the early years of the thirteenth century, although this is not certain for it could equally well date from the end of the century.[1] Its connection with the Order of Templars makes one wonder if this keep would not have certain features reminiscent of the style of building in the Holy Land. Its very simple rectangular plan, with four square towers at each corner, is typical of the Byzantine fortresses, which were copied in Syria from the middle of the twelfth century onwards in the Frankish castles of Blanche-Garde (near Jerusalem) and Giblet (south of Tripoli); but there is little evidence that this plan was followed in the keeps, although it is true that one side of the great rectangular tower at Tortosa (built by the Templars) has square towers at each corner. The interior design of the Temple is more noticeably similar to that of the square keep at Saone in Syria, where the rooms are ceiled by panels of ribbed vaulting supported on a central pillar. But although these similarities are worth

---

[1] Henri de Curzon (*La maison du Temple de Paris*, pp. 120–22) points out the difficulty in dating this building.

noting it would be unwise to exaggerate their importance. (Fig. 3.)

The great revival in military architecture was led, as one would naturally expect, by the powerful kings and princes of the time; by the sons of William the Conquerer and their descendants, the Plantagenets, when they became dukes of Normandy. These were the men who built all the most typical twelfth-century fortified castles remaining today.

Gisors (Eure) was one of the frontier posts on the Epte river dividing the Duchy of Normandy from the royal domains of France. Its castle is still in a remarkable state of preservation: the keep, the chemise and the bailey wall are practically intact.

An examination of the masonry shows quite clearly the successive stages of its construction; the stone facing of the chemise, or the surrounding wall, and of the lower floors of the keep is rather coarse, but it is much finer in the upper floors of the keep, the buttresses, and in several doors. From the three available sources of information it is possible to throw some light on the somewhat obscure history of the original building. The chronicler, Robert de Torigni (alias Robert du Mont) records that William Rufus (1087–1100) built Gisors in 1096, and that his brother, Henry I (1100–35) made the castle impregnable by surrounding it by walls and high towers (*Williamus fecit . . . Gisorth . . . quod . . . frater ejus Henricus . . . moenibus ambitum et turribus excelsis inexpugnabile reddidit*). Orderic Vital states that the castle was founded in 1097 and adds that William Rufus had it built by the engineer, Robert de Bellême. Thirdly, Robert de Torigni refers to Gisors in 1123 as being one of the castles founded by Henry I Beauclerc (*sic etiam fecit castellum Gisorz*). In the *Bulletin monumental*, 1958, M. Yves Bruand gives what would appear to be the correct interpretation of these three documents. From the absence of any towers on the keep or on the chemise, he concludes that these were built by Robert de Bellême at about 1096 or 1097. On the other hand the presence of towers on the great bailey-wall leads him to conclude that this was built by Henry I in 1123. In view of the relatively short lapse of time between 1096–97 and 1123, the fact that the stonework is of equally rough quality throughout does not invalidate his conclusions. In the light of this assumption we can now make a closer study of the oldest existing sections of the castle, that is to say, the lower two floors of the keep (excluding the buttresses), the chemise wall (also excluding the buttresses) and practically the whole of the outer wall.

The keep and its chemise, erected by Robert de Bellême on an artificial mound 60 feet high, are typical of the eleventh-century castles of the period; they have no buttresses and the interior of the keep has neither vaulting nor any stone staircase. But they present certain new features that are worth noting. In the first place the octagonal keep is one of the earliest, perhaps the first of its kind at that time, and was probably adopted to conform with the principles laid down by Vitruvius (I. 5) to the effect that the circular or polygonal keep was superior to the rectangular type. Seccndly, a number of wooden beams are bedded in the rubble of the chemise to reinforce the cementing of the masonry; this also follows principles recommended by Vitruvius (1, 5) and Philo of Byzantium (III, 3). Finally, the entrance is sited at the point of junction of the keep and the chemise; a narrow, barrel-vaulted passage cut in the thickness of the chemise leads to the courtyard; the entrance to the keep (now walled up) is at the point where this passage emerges. The entrance therefore (contrary to usual practice at that time) was actually on the ground floor, but was so deeply set in the angle between the keep and the chemise wall that it was practically impossible to force it. This was no doubt the first example of an entrance protected by a narrow approaching tunnel. Some years later the keep at Houdan was designed on an amended version of the same principle.

It is worth noting that, in spite of these novel features, the system of defence of Gisors castle in 1096 or 1097 showed no real advance upon that of its predecessors; it relied entirely upon the strength of the walls and the difficulty of access. But the building of the outer wall in 1123 was to give a completely new character to the place.

This outer wall, of which the southern section has now completely disappeared, surrounds the keep at a distance of about one hundred yards. Robert de Torigni's expression, *turribus excelsis* suggests that its towers stood high above the curtain and could therefore cover it by their flanking fire; this is the outstanding feature of the outer wall. Of all the French castles still standing, Gisors was almost the first to demonstrate the application of the great principle enumerated by Vegetius (IV, 2) of bringing flanking fire on to the walls; and it was followed at Gisors far more intelligently than at Houdan. The space between the towers at Gisors is no greater than the range of the weapons of the time, and they are open at the gorges[1] in order to deny cover to any attackers who might capture them. Having carried the first obstacle the exhausted besiegers would therefore find themselves without cover, completely dominated by the immense fire-power from the keep. It is clear, therefore, that the science of fortification was no longer static, it had become an organised system of defence with its various parts properly co-ordinated and mutually interdependent.

Most of the towers of the outer wall of 1123 were square. On the west side three of them are reinforced externally by solid masses of masonry of which some have the form of the segment of a circle with the round edge to the front, while others are triangular, the apex forming a pointed spur facing outwards. This spur-shaped design has the double advantage of fending off projectiles from siege engines and of increasing the difficulty of sapping; but it also denotes the application of one of the principles laid down by Philo of Byzantium (1, 2 and 4) to the effect that polygon-shaped towers should be so sited as to present a protruding angular surface capable of deflecting projectiles. These protruding spurs or prows became quite common on keeps of the late twelfth century (notably at La Roche-Guyon, at Issoudun, and at the Château-Gaillard); M. Ives Burand therefore suggests that the reinforcement of the Gisors towers was a later addition; he admits, however, that the stonework is of the same coarse quality as that of the towers themselves. One is tempted to make the somewhat rash suggestion that it was Henry I (who died in 1135) who was responsible for this new

---

[1] Two of these were closed later as a result of modifications made during the reign of Phillip-Augustus (cf. Louis Regnier *Quelques mots sur Gisors*, p. 27).

idea, and that he put it into practice for the first time at Gisors.

After having been ceded to France for some years during the Wars of the Roses, Gisors became a Norman castle again in 1161, by the marriage of Henry II's son with the daughter of Louis VII. Robert de Torigni's chronicles record that Henry II also ordered the Normandy frontier posts to be repaired and restored; particularly Gisors (*et maxime Gisorz*). The great register of the Normandy Exchequer for the year 1180 and particularly for 1184 (*Mémoires de la Société des Antiquaires de Normandie*, 1846, pp. 23, 34, 36 and 37) also mentions a number of quite considerable sums expended on Gisors, notably (in 1184) for the roofing of the keep, a lock on the gate, and for other unspecified work carried out on the chemise and the kitchen housed in it.

The work done on the castle by Henry II Plantagenet was in fact considerably more important than these few entries would suggest. It is easily recognisable by the high quality of the stonework, in sharp contrast to the rough masonry of the older parts of the building. Two well-lit floors with semi-circular window-openings were added to the keep, which at the same time was strengthened by seven massive buttresses of a much heavier type than the flat buttresses usually found in Norman keeps; so thick, in fact, that a spiral staircase could be cut in one of them between the first and second floors.[1] Buttresses were also added to the chemise, although they project but slightly; and it must have been at this time that the existing gate was built. It was approached from the bailey by a straight flight of steps between two walls following the slope of the motte. One is immediately reminded of the almost identical type of stairway leading to the keep at Conisbrough in Yorkshire and attributed by Geo. T. Clark to Henry II's stepbrother, Hamelin Plantagenet (1163–1201). Note in passing that it was very probably Prince Hamelin who built the chapel of atonement dedicated to Saint Thomas à Becket, who was canonised in 1173. The apse of this chapel can still be seen, built into the curtain wall.

---

[1] No connection with the wide vice built in the turret adjoining the keep; this was added during the second half of the fourteenth century, if not later.

Henry II's influence is also clearly recognisable in two
additions to the bailey-wall. The first is the Devil's Tower on
the north side, which has rib-vaulting on two floors. This
tower shows a great advance on those of 1123: it projects
boldly beyond the line of the curtain wall; its plan is semicircular; and the arrow-loops are 'staggered' from floor to
floor so as to avoid excessive strain on any one part of the
walls. The second is in the Governor's Tower at the south-east
corner, which was already standing. The changes made here
are easily visible: the entrance passage, 15 feet long, has
barrel-vaulting in its western half (that is, on the inside) and
rib-vaulting on the other (that is, on the outside) half.
Eugène Pepin explains this very clearly by pointing out that
the inside half of the passage represents the original entrance
belonging to the curtain wall built in 1123; the outer half of
the passage lies against the Governor's Tower, added later
to strengthen the whole building at this point; and the
Governor's Tower has the same characteristics as the Devil's
Tower: it is rounded on the outside, loopholed in the same
manner, with rib-vaulting on the first floor. The upper
floors and the door of the Tower, however, which have
pointed vaulting, were a later addition by Phillip-Augustus.

In contrast to Gisors, no records are available for a detailed
study of Niort (Deux Sevres). We must therefore be content
if we can place the castle in its correct historical context. Its
relatively later type rules out any possibility that it was built
very early in the twelfth century; on the other hand certain
details, such as the absence of plinths at the foot of the walls
and the narrow span of the Norman arches in the bays, prevent any rash assumption that it was of much later date.
Niort is in the former province of Poitou, which formed part
of the domain of Eleanor of Aquitaine, married to Louis VII
in 1137, divorced in 1152 and married immediately afterwards to Henry II Plantagenet, who became King of England
two years later and died in 1189. It must have been either
Louis VII or Henry II who built the present castle. But
Louis was no great builder of castles; and, indeed, according
to local tradition recorded in the eighteenth century, the
keep was built by the English and Eleanor lived in it. If so,
it must have been built by Henry II. A good deal could be

said in support of this legend. Alfred Richard, in his *Histoire des comtes de Poitou*, p. 176, tries to be more definite and puts forward the quite unsubstantiated claim that the fortress was built after Eleanor and her sons had rebelled against Henry II in 1174. All we are prepared to say, in the light of the evidence available, is that it seems reasonable to date the building of Niort in the third quarter of the twelfth century.

The castle consisted of a keep standing in the middle of a vast bailey. The bailey-wall has disappeared, but our knowledge of it comes from a number of eighteenth-century drawings, of which the most important is kept in the print-room[1] of the French National Library (Va 38b). This is a large wash-tint measuring 21½ inches by 31 inches, showing the curtain with its sixteen towers, ten of which have open gorges like those at Gisors; but they are an improvement on the Gisors tower in that they are round on the outside, whereas the towers at Niort are square.

The keep is surrounded by a moat, and has the almost unique distinction of being double. It is formed by twin towers joined by two curtains which originally enclosed a courtyard. In the fifteenth century this courtyard was roofed in to provide living quarters. The north tower collapsed in 1749 and was at once rebuilt; but the foundations and the lower courses were preserved, and the masons' marks are seen to be the same as those on the twin tower; a proof that both were built at the same time.

The initial advantage of the double keep was that if one tower were captured the defence could still be carried on in the other. We are inclined to think, however, that it was part of a more subtle and ingenious plan derived from the principle of the double gate, briefly referred to by Vegetius (IV, 4) and well known in classical times; the so-called black gate at Trèves is a good example. Two powerful towers are joined together by a double line of buildings with an open courtyard between them. Each building has a gate leading from the outside into the courtyard. If one gate is forced the attackers enter the courtyard but are held up at the second gate. The portcullis of the first gate is then dropped behind

[1] Cabinet des Estampes de Paris.

IV *The Castle, La Brède*

them and the men shut inside the courtyard come under heavy attack from all sides. Similarly at Niort, any attackers foolhardy enough to force their way into the open courtyard would find themselves in a trap and be wiped out by the fire from the two keeps. It would appear that the entrance to the castle was originally a postern gate in the eastern curtain at the height of the first floor, where a turret flanks the wall. Access to the two keeps was along the curtain, and one entered the keeps – as was usual – at first-floor level.

The keeps themselves are square towers with four round turrets; possibly the first of their kind. They are reinforced, as at Loches, with semicircular buttresses applied at the middle of each façade. A strikingly novel feature is the addition of stone machicolations on the north and south sides of the southern (that is, the older) tower in the form of wide, keyed-in arches projecting slightly beyond the wall between the centre buttress and the corner turrets. Machicoulis of this type were first used in the Holy Land. They make their appearance at Saone in the first half of the twelfth century in the form of an arch over a gateway, following – so it is said – a principle laid down by Vegetius (IV, 4). A group of three appears a little later on the north-west prow of the Krac des Chevaliers. M. Paul Deschamps (*Crac des Chevaliers*, p. 279) takes the view that they 'belong to the earlier Frankish parts of the castle', that is to say, to the middle of the twelfth century, if not earlier. In the west, the arch-type of machicolation is found at the castle of Ghent, erected by Phillip of Alsace in 1180, at Lucheux (Somme) dating, according to M. Paul Deschamps, from 1192 (*Congrès archéologique*, 1936, p. 264), and at Château-Gaillard, which was built very late in the twelfth century. It is very probable, therefore, that those at Niort were the first seen in France.

When Richard Coeur de Lion returned from the Third Crusade in 1194, he found Phillip-Augustus in possession of the places and lands ceded to him by King John. By the treaty of Issoudun (December 5th, 1195) Richard agreed to ratify the cession of Gisors, but he set to work immediately to compensate for its loss by building Château-Gaillard at Les Andelys (Eure) in order to cover the approaches to Rouen (see frontispiece).

v *The Castle, Tarascon*   D

The chronicler John Brampton claims that this fortress, which was considered to be the greatest of all Norman castles, was completed in one year. According to Brampton, Richard was so delighted that he exclaimed: 'a wonderful girl indeed! – and but twelve months old!' Sidney Toy, however, (*History of Fortification*, p. 128) points out that Brampton's chronicles are certainly not of an earlier date than the middle of the fourteenth century and are therefore unreliable. What is more, the great roll of the Normandy Exchequer for 1198 (Stapleton edition, II, pp. 309–10) shows that work on Château-Gaillard was well in hand two years before; it must therefore have begun in 1196. Mr. Sidney Toy even questions the possibility of the keep having been completed during Richard's lifetime. It is certainly strange that when Phillip-Augustus attacked the castle in 1204, its defenders fled as soon as the last remaining curtain wall was forced, and made no attempt at a last stand in the keep itself.

Marcel Dieulafoy, in *Mémoires Académie des Inscriptions*, 1898, considers that the building of Château-Gaillard opened a new era in the art of fortification; if our reading of him is correct, Mr. Sidney Toy (p. 128), is of the same opinion. On page 344, Marcel Dieulafoy writes: 'We witness the dramatic appearance of an entirely new principle, foreign in its conception, but enormously effective; and its origin, I submit, is to be sought in Syria and Palestine.' We find it difficult to accept this view and would suggest that Château-Gaillard marks the end of an era, not the beginning of a new one. In the preceding pages we have tried to show the steady development of ideas in military architecture from the beginning of the twelfth century onwards as the result of the knowledge gleaned from the ancient writers during the Crusades by the military commanders of the West. Detailed study of Château-Gaillard will show that most of its characteristic features had already appeared in earlier French castles, and one is forced to the conclusion that Château-Gaillard was the final expression of all the progress made in the design and construction of fortified castles during the Norman period.

Its site is similar to that of Loches. The fortress stands on a promontory with precipitous slopes on all sides but one, where it is connected by an isthmus to the line of hills of which it forms part. But whereas the keep at Loches stands on the isthmus itself and is the sole protection of the vast bailey covering the inaccessible plateau behind it, the keep at Château-Gaillard is at the extreme end of the promontory; it is, therefore, the last retreat of the defence system, and can only be reached when a whole series of co-ordinated defence-works covering it has been captured. This plan was not, however, entirely original; it was used, notably, at La Roche-Guyon (Seine-et-Oise), which is on the Seine about twenty to twenty-five miles above Les Andelys. La Roche-Guyon is a little older than Château-Gaillard, and has a number of similar features that are worth considering.

In front of the castle itself a wide ditch was cut through the isthmus; beyond this was a defensive outwork with wall-towers, covering the fortress on the one side exposed to possible attack. Chinon stands on a site similar to that of La Roche Guyon, and was built (according to Cougny and Eugène Pepin) by Henry II Plantagenet. On exactly the same principle as at La Roche-Guyon, the St. George fort pro-tected Chinon on the plateau side. At both places – the one in Normandy and the other in Touraine – the only means of access to the outer fort was by crossing the moat and entering by a gate on the inner side of the fort. Guillaume le Breton, describing the siege of Château-Gaillard in 1204 (*Philippide VII*, verses 790–91), tells us that the approach to this outer fort at Château-Gaillard was by a pulley-type drawbridge over the moat (*Funibus abruptus pontis versatilis axem inversum . . . se sternere cogit*).

The general plan of the castle itself is remarkably similar to that of La Roche-Guyon. The three main structures, keep, chemise and bailey-wall, lie on the same axis, and are strategically interdependent. Although its exact date is not known, La Roche-Guyon has certain features suggesting that it is older than Château-Gaillard; no provision is made for flanking the curtains, and knowledge of machicolation seems to have been lacking.

Château-Gaillard has a far more comprehensive system of defence. The towers on the outer bailey project to an unusual degree beyond the line of the wall. The ultimate stronghold, consisting of the keep and the chemise, is protected by a moat. The plan of the chemise is also unusual; it consists of a line of semicircular towers set so closely together that the curtains between them are but 3 feet long. It will be remembered, however, that this apparently new feature is merely a development of the type of curtain we noticed on the keeps at Etampes and Ambleny.

Finally, the keep itself is a round tower with walls 12 feet thick and a prow-shaped projection like the keep at La Roche-Guyon. Round its crest were machicolations of the keyed-arch type supported on buttresses embedded in a stone plinth reinforcing the base of the walls. Similar plinths were used in conjunction with machicolations on castles of earlier date than Château-Gaillard; mention has already been made of them at the Krac des Chevaliers and at Lucheux. It would appear that the original purpose of the plinth was to increase the effect of machicolation; which supports Brutails' suggestion (*Précis d'archéologie*, pp. 235–36) that the object of the plinth was not so much to counteract sapping as to deflect projectiles thrown down from the walls above. Marcel Dieulafoy (p. 332) remarks that the upper part of the plinth of the keep at Château-Gaillard is concave and the lower part oblique; the effect therefore would be to deflect projectiles into a fan-shaped trajectory.

Our study of this castle should lead us to the conclusion already suggested that Château-Gaillard is the final embodiment of all the progress made in fortification during the twelfth century; it is the crowning example of a fortified castle of the Norman era.

4 | The Phillip-Augustus Formula

On March 6th, 1204, five years after Richard Coeur de Lion's death, Phillip-Augustus at last succeeded in taking the castle of Château-Gaillard. The moral effect of the capture of this reputedly impregnable fortress was shattering; two months later the whole of Normandy had been conquered.

In order to establish his authority over the lands thus restored to the Crown, Phillip-Augustus took steps to strengthen the existing castles and, where necessary, to build new ones.

To the castles already standing Phillip was content to add new keeps, sited to cover the most vulnerable side of the castle; notable examples are the Prisoners' Tower at Gisors, the Talbot Tower at Falaise, and the Coudray Tower at Chinon. The plan of these keeps follows familiar lines; they are well-masoned circular towers 40 to 45 feet in diameter with massive walls up to 12 feet thick, battered at the base; the spiral stairs are built in the thickness of the wall, turning alternately from right to left and from left to right at each floor. The arrow-loops are cut on an irregular pattern in order to avoid weakening the wall by setting them one above the other; the rooms have pointed vaulting throughout, thereby greatly reducing the risk of fire. At Gisors, Falaise, and Chinon the entrance is on the level of the top of the adjoining curtain, that is to say, at the third floor.

The most important of the new castles built by Phillip-Augustus were the Louvre and Rouen; all that remains of them today is the keep (the Joan-of-Arc Tower) at Rouen. Yèvre-le-Chatel and Dourdan, although admittedly less famous, are sufficiently intact to give some idea of the typical Phillip-Augustus castle. They were clearly far simpler than those of the Plantagenets, for they consist of a plain rectangular keep, flanked by round towers, and a bailey with a protecting wall. Following the practice in many of the Normandy castles (and particularly at Gisors) the living accommodation, formerly in the keep, has been installed in a more comfortable and better-lit building. But while this building stands in the bailey at Gisors – outside the chemise – it is located within the courtyard of the keeps at Yèvre-le-Châtel and Dourdan. The castle has ceased, in fact, to be essentially a fortress; it is developing into a fortified palace.

Yèvre-le-Châtel (Loiret) is a small castle in the Gothic style, but certain older features, such as a number of round arches in the openings, should prevent underestimating its age: M. Jean Vallery-Radot (*Congrès archéologique*, 1930) is inclined to date it very early in the thirteenth century (p. 56).

It is a diamond-shaped building with towers at each corner;

each side measuring about one hundred feet. The towers have a diameter of 31 feet and are of about equal strength. This castle follows the Byzantine model in having no keep; the towers are similar in plan to those described above; they are circular, battered at the base, and have similar arrow-loops; the staircases are built in the thickness of the walls in the manner of those at Gisors; the rooms are hexagonal and have six-panelled pointed vaulting. As a protection against sapping the towers have solid bases. They are cut through at the height of the curtains in order to provide a continuous passage on the wall-walk so that the garrison, in case of an attack, could quickly concentrate at the point threatened. It is important to note that these two features – the solid wall-bases and the continuous wall-walk – are also to be seen in the Gallo-Roman chemise at Senlis.

An outstanding particularity of the masonry of the curtains is that it is reinforced with wide relieving arches keyed into the towers on either side. This device is intended to counteract the possible effects of sapping, for even if the base of the walls were destroyed the wall itself would still be supported by the relieving arch. This principle was unquestionably borrowed from the Byzantines; it was used by Justinian in the sixth century and Enlart reports an example of it still visible on the ramparts at Salonica. The entrance, as usual, is well above ground-level and is protected by the tower beside it; it was approached by a bridge resting on a stone plinth at the far side. On each side of the gate are two grooved corbels obviously designed to carry the swivel-pins of a drawbridge. The gateway passage was strongly defended, first by a fall-trap, then by a portcullis, and finally by a second gate, forming a combined system of defence based on the principles of Vegetius (IV, 4); an example earlier than that of Yèvre-le-Châtel has already been mentioned at Giblet (Tripoli), built by the Crusaders during the first half of the twelfth century.

The living quarters are built against the west curtain inside the courtyard and are quite extensive, occupying nearly half of the courtyard. The great hall on the ground floor was divided in the middle by a line of arches carried on columns with foliated capitals.

VI *Azay-le-Rideau*

Dourdan (Seine-et-Oise) must have been built towards the end of the reign of Phillip-Augustus (1180–1223). In a deed dated 1222 (see p. 56), the King describes it as his 'new castle of Dourdan'.

Although of later date, it has close points of resemblance with the Louvre, of which the great tower at least was certainly completed in 1202. Both castles were built on an almost square plan and had comparable dimensions; the Louvre, 240 feet by 225 feet, Dourdan (slightly trapezoidal) 200 feet by 220 feet; both were surrounded by moats and flanked by towers at each corner. In both castles a tower was added at the middle of each wall in order to bring the whole area of the curtains within the effective range of flanking fire, and the width between the towers was thereby reduced to about one hundred feet. This plan follows the principle laid down by Vitruvius (I, 5), and is seen on the chemise at Senlis. At Dourdan the gate is sited between twin towers in the middle of one wall, the towers serving the dual purpose of guarding the gate and flanking the curtains on either side. All these auxiliary towers, of course, are circular, battered at the base and pierced with arrow-loops. At Dourdan their walls and the curtain walls are 9 feet thick; the rooms have pointed vaulting, and the corner towers project boldly beyond the line of the wall in order to ensure maximum flanking effect. Both at the Louvre and at Dourdan the keeps had separate moats around them and were more powerfully built than the other towers. The diameter of the Louvre keep was 50 feet; that at Dourdan 45 feet. But whereas at the Louvre the keep stood inside the courtyard – probably taking up far too much of the space available – at Dourdan it took the place of one of the corner towers at the point most exposed to possible attack. This keep still stands some 80 feet high; its masonry is of very high standard; the walls are over 12 feet thick and carry spiral staircases of the 'alternating' type, that is to say, reversing their turn from right to left or left to right from floor to floor; and the rooms have six-pointed panelled vaulting. Its most striking feature, however, is the position of the door, which, like the Joan-of-Arc Tower at Rouen, is on the ground floor and opens on to the courtyard at the same level. Facing it is another door leading outside. Military

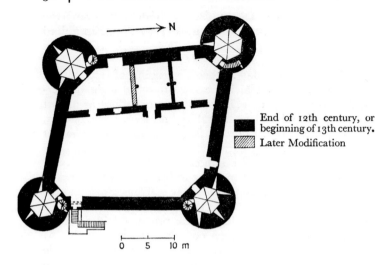

End of 12th century, or
beginning of 13th century.
Later Modification

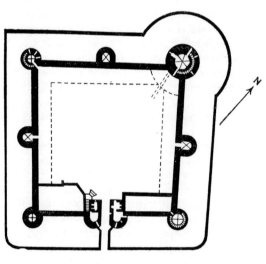

FIG. 2 *(above)* YÈVRE-LE-CHÂTEL *(congrès archéologique, 1930)*.
(below) DOURDAN *(congrès archéologique, 1944)*.

engineers had now become aware of the disadvantage of siting doors high above the ground; the besieged garrison is shut up inside a tower and cannot get out. The policy of bringing doors down to ground-level shows that the static system of defence was a thing of the past.

Looked at as a whole, the castles built by Phillip-Augustus derive their chief merit from the clarity and simplicity of the plans he adopted. These qualities were the fruit of the knowledge the King had acquired from a very comprehensive study of the writers of antiquity. His use, for example, of the portcullis or the fall-trap in the defence of gateways, or his insistence on the correct distance between towers, show how thoroughly he had absorbed the ancient learning. But it is clear also that he had studied the ancient monuments themselves. The four-sided plan with corner towers comes from the Byzantine fortresses; the Crusaders copied it towards the middle of the twelfth century adding a central keep – and used it at Blanche-Garde and Giblet. It seems likely also that Phillip-Augustus had studied the remains of the Gallo-Roman forts in his own domains, particularly the curtain wall at Senlis, which in his time was almost intact (Louis XI had it demolished in the fifteenth century). It is quite possible that Phillip-Augustus's use of circular towers with a solid base and of a continuous wall-walk round the curtain was the result of these studies.

Phillip-Augustus undoubtedly took full advantage of the progress being made at the time in the art of building, as is shown by the use of pointed vaulting (which made stone ceilings possible on every floor) and by the irregular siting of arrow-loops (an idea borrowed from castles in the south of France). But it is noticeable that he did not adopt the use of stone machicolation, probably because the only machicolation known to the West at that time was of the arch type, mounted on buttresses that might hinder flanking fire. Phillip-Augustus therefore continued to use hoards in his castles. In Jean de Berry's Book of Hours ('*Les Tres Riches Heures du Duc de Berry*') at Chantilly the month of April is illuminated with a painting of the castle at Dourdan showing the hoards round the keep.

M. Raymond Ritter points out (p. 40) that the formula

used by Phillip-Augustus in designing the castles described above had its origin – its archetype – nearly three-quarters of a century earlier in the castle of Carcassonne, built by the Trencavel family in 1130. Although Carcassonne retains the general characteristics of the 'Norman' style – as shown by the absence of pointed vaulting – its rectangular plan, 264 feet by 132 feet, is conspicuously simple; the towers are circular, battered at the base and set close together to ensure adequate flanking of the curtains; the arrow-loops are 'staggered'; the lower floors are ceiled with dome vaulting; the gate stands between twin towers and the approach passage to it is defended by a fall-trap, a portcullis, and a second gate; there is no keep, and the living quarters are inside the courtyard.

There can be no question, therefore, as to the affinity between Carcassonne and the castles of Phillip-Augustus. But it is extremely difficult to understand what direct relationship could have existed between them. We think that in fact there was no such relationship, for Carcassonne was not brought under the French Crown until the reign of Louis VIII. The explanation would seem to be that Carcassonne and the castles of Phillip-Augustus shared the same source of inspiration; the Kings of France had the Gallo-Roman curtain wall at Senlis for a model; the Trencavels had the Visigothic *enceinte* at Carcassonne under their eyes to complete the knowledge they had gained during the Crusades. Working from similar models it was not surprising that they arrived at similar results. At the risk of over-simplification, one may reasonably conclude that the formula followed by both Phillip-Augustus on the one hand and the Trencavel rulers on the other, was the expression of a return to the ancient texts.

The results of the policy initiated by the King were soon apparent in the most famous French castle of the Middle Ages at Coucy (Aisne). It was built during the minority of Saint Louis during the second quarter of the thirteenth century by Enguerrand III, 'Sire de Coucy'.[1] The fortress

---

[1] The motto of the Coucy family was: '*Roy ne suis, ne prince, ne duc, ne comte aussy; Je suis Sire de Coucy.*'

is immensely powerful and of imposing dimensions. The keep is 180 feet high and has a diameter of some 102 feet; the thickness of the walls at ground level is 24 feet. Until its destruction in 1917 it was reputed to be the greatest of all known keeps. Compared with such a giant, the Louvre, measuring only 50 feet in diameter, seems puny indeed.

But on closer examination we find that from the military point of view it has no novel features. Its plan is an irregular quadrilateral (following the configuration of the site); it has four massive corner towers, with diameters ranging from 57 to 63 feet and walls up to 16 feet thick on the south side where the entrance stands; the towers are battered at the base and the various floors have six-panelled pointed vaulting; the keep is surrounded by a wide ditch and stands astride one of the walls, as at Rouen; it has a solid, battered base and a door on the ground floor; its rooms have twelve-panelled pointed vaulting on every floor, and the living quarters back on to the inside of the curtain. It is, in fact, an enlarged version of one of Phillip-Augustus's castles. It has, however, one feature which is absent from the royal castles; the keep and the three other towers are crowned with stone corbels on which wooden hoards could be fitted. This might suggest an attempt to copy the stone machicolation mounted on consoles in the Frankish fortresses in Syria at that time; but there are two good reasons for thinking otherwise. In the first place it is not at all certain, in our view, that parapets for machicolation mounted on consoles were in use in the Frankish fortresses of the Holy Land as early as the first half of the thirteenth century. M. Paul Deschamps (*Crac des Chevaliers*, p. 265) is of the opinion that this type of machicolation was only built on to the Krac des Chevaliers after its capture by the Mohammedans in 1271. The second reason is that small stone corbels had already been in use in France many years before to carry the beams supporting the hoards. Reference has already been made to hoards of this type at Gisors and Chambois as early as the twelfth century, and at Montségur (Ariège) in the first thirty years of the thirteenth century. Other later examples can be quoted up to the closing years of the century, such as Rozemont (Nièvre) and Blanquefort (Gironde). The only peculiarity of the corbels at Coucy is that they are larger than those elsewhere: they have four quarter-circles in the moulding whereas others have only two.

Like Coucy, the great castle of Boulogne-sur-Mer dates from the minority of Saint Louis; like Coucy also it was an expression of defiance of the royal authority by a powerful feudal lord. An old inscription, long since vanished, states that it was built in 1231 by Phillip Hurepel – an uncle of Saint Louis – who joined a coalition of the great vassals against the King in 1228, but who made his submission in 1230 and died soon after, in 1234. It seems likely, in view of these circumstances, that 1231 was the date on which the castle was actually finished.

Like Coucy again, Boulogne shows clearly the influence of Phillip-Augustus. It is built on an irregular octagonal plan and is surrounded by a moat. The cylindrical corner towers are solid at the base; for the most part they have semi-dome vaulting on each floor and are pierced with 'staggered' arrow-loops, which originally flanked the curtains. It follows Yèvre-le-Châtel in having no keep – a novel omission at that time. Inside the courtyard – measuring 40 yards by 33 yards – were living quarters built against the whole available wall space. Of these the lower room with its pointed vaulting is still standing; above it was the great hall, which had an open timber roof and four handsome windows looking out on the courtyard. Like Yèvre-le-Châtel again, Boulogne is an example of the principle of the continuous wall-walk; it passes behind the great hall and the chapel beside it; but it is cleverly arranged to open out as it passes through the armoury, forming a gallery from which the officers could keep an eye on their men.

Blanche de Castille could not prevent her feudal vassals from building themselves castles on an equally grand scale to that of Coucy or Boulogne, but she also built a considerable number herself. At Angers, in the heart of the lands conquered from the Plantagenets, she undertook the erection of one of the greatest fortresses in the kingdom. There can be no doubt that it was she who was personally responsible for this enterprise for, from the records of sums paid out in compensation for expropriation, it is clear that building operations began in 1232 during her regency; they apparently continued until 1238, that is to say, after the accession of Louis IX (Saint Louis). (See Plate 1.)

Angers had been the home of the Counts of Anjou since the middle of the ninth century. The old palace had been rebuilt after a fire, but on the side facing the River Maine a fragment of one of the original walls is still visible; it is faced with small stone (*opus constructum lapillis*), and seems to date from the end of the eleventh or the beginning of the twelfth century. But for all intents and purposes this immense castle stands today as it was when it was built during the reign of Saint Louis.

The surrounding wall follows a mitre-shaped plan with the short (straight) side to the north-west, overhanging the River Maine. M. Henri René tells us that the total length of the perimeter is 1047 yards. Before the present riverside embankment was built (between 1783 and 1842) the walls rose sheer from the river-bed. There are no towers on this north-west side; the other sides are flanked by seventeen heavy circular towers battered at the base, with arrow-loops on the 'staggered' principle already described. There is no keep. The towers were originally much higher than they are today. By letters patent dated November 7th, 1585, Henry III gave authority to the governor to demolish the fortification of the castle. But, in fact, the governor did far more to modernise than to destroy it: he was content to lower the height of the towers to the level of the top of the curtains by suppressing the upper floors; he also built a platform over the 'Field Gate', which led out into the open country. The surrounding wall was built of shale available on the actual site – sound material, but flat and friable – bonded with horizontal courses of limestone; and it is these alternate layers of black and white stone which give the castle its characteristic appearance.

Saint Louis came of age in 1235. From this date onwards – except for the short struggle against the English King, Henry III (marked by the French victory of Saintes in 1242) and Philippe le Bel's[1] campaign against the Flemish at the

[1] King Phillip IV (1285–1314).

beginning of the fourteenth century, the kingdom of France enjoyed peace for a hundred years. The authority of the Capetian dynasty was sufficiently great to repress the turbulence of the feudal lords, and the building of fortified places was exclusively the business of the Crown. When Count Raymond of Toulouse died in 1249, his lands came into the possession of Saint Louis' brother, Alphonse de Poitiers, who had married Count Raymond's only daughter. The people of Najac, alarmed at the possible threat of being annexed by the Crown, took up arms against what they considered to be foreign domination. The revolt was suppressed in 1250, and Alphonse de Poitiers forestalled further trouble by considerably strengthening the castle. The date of the work is revealed by a letter dated February 21st, 1253, from the Seneschal of Rouergue, telling Alphonse de Poitiers that he had bought lime, engaged masons, and was making the necessary preparations for work to begin. It is thought that the earlier fortress was built at the beginning of the twelfth century. The considerable part of it still standing is built of shale rubble and drift boulders from Aveyron, and is easily distinguished from the fine stone used during the restoration carried out in the thirteenth century. The twelfth-century castle had two equal sides 120 feet long and two unequal sides of 78 feet and 63 feet respectively. The south-west corner was fortified by a square keep of probably earlier date than the curtains. When Alphonse de Poitiers set out to modernise the castle he adopted the same procedure as his grandfather, Phillip-Augustus, would have done.

The castle is perched on a rocky promontory hemmed in by the Aveyron river 300 feet below. It has no moat – for the very good reason that at such a height no water was available; but the height of the old walls was raised very considerably. At the same time all the floors of the keep were ceiled with pointed vaulting. Finally, the north, east and south sides were flanked with circular towers, their rooms also being ceiled with pointed vaulting. The tower at the south-east corner, which was much stronger than the others, served the purpose of a keep placed at the most vulnerable point of the castle in exactly the same way as the keeps added by Phillip-Augustus at Falaise, Chinon, and elsewhere. The

Governor's house was in the courtyard, against the western curtain.

A great deal of thought was given to the details of the defence plan. Except in the new keep there was no direct communication between the floors of the towers. The only access to the top floor was along the wall-walk on the crest of the curtains, and this was reached by climbing open stairways built against the walls and completely exposed to defensive fire. This shows an improvement upon the similar arrangement at Dourdan, where the upper floors of the towers in the middle of the curtains could only be reached along the wall-walk. Several points should be noted, also, in regard to the arrow-loops. By the middle of the fifteenth century, the 'staggered' pattern was common practice; but in addition, it is interesting to find at Najac a line of arrow-loops at the base of the walls; this was an innovation in northern France at the time and may well have been copied from Carcassonne, where it had already been in use since the second quarter of the twelfth century. It is noticeable also that the arrow-loops in the new keep are unusually long – 22 feet – due to the very steep downward deflection of the lower sill, the object being to allow the archer to shoot almost vertically on to the foot of the wall. This same feature exists in the Constance Tower at Aigues-Mortes, which is of approximately the same date. Following the usual practice at that time, the castle was surmounted by hoards; some of the put-log holes for the supporting beams are still to be seen around the new keep and on the south curtain. But at the top of the keep is a stone brattice sited to cover two doors in the lower floors immediately below. Brattices were small shelters built out on corbels or consoles but without foot-boards; they were used from earliest times as latrines; one can be seen on the keep at La Roche-Posay (Vienne), dating from the beginning of the twelfth century. Two other examples of brattices referred to by Eugène Lefèvre-Pontalis in his book on Coucy (pp. 43 and 66) were also used as latrines. In the Holy Land the Crusaders had the idea of using these small shelters as hoards; and at the Krac des Chevaliers, for example, a number of them can be seen, lined up on the west face of the inner wall. At Najac, however, the siting of the brattice at the top of the wall immediately above two doors leaves no doubt as to its military purpose; and it is perhaps the earliest example of this type of defence to be found in any French castle.

4 | Foreign Castles on French Soil

The building of privately-owned fortified castles within France itself was halted during the hundred years peace; but a number of castles appeared on the borders of the kingdom on lands that were in fact alien enclaves, although in theory they were under the suzerainty of the King.

Philippe Lauzun has made a study of a number of minor fortresses in the Gers, located – as he points out – on either side of the frontier between the provinces of Agenais and Armagnac. He notes that two of these – La Gardère and Sainte Mère – probably date from the last quarter of the thirteenth century; and he concludes that all these forts were built immediately after the cession of Agenais to England by the Treaty of Amiens in 1279; some by Edward I and the others by the Count of Armagnac.

These small fortified structures – which are all very much alike – can hardly be described as castles. Philippe Lauzun quotes, as typical examples, Le Tauzia, Massencôme, La Gardère and the tower at Le Guardès, near Valence-sur-Baise. They stand on high ground and are rectangular buildings 50 to 65 feet long by 35 to 60 feet wide; their masonry is of good, medium-size stone; and they are flanked by two square turrets usually sited at diagonally opposite corners. The interior arrangement is somewhat rudimentary. Communication between the four storeys (which have wooden floors) is by ladder only; the only lighting in the ground and first floors is by the loopholes; the second floor has twin lights; and a crenellated wall-walk runs along the top floor at the height of the gutters. The entrance is either by a gateway on the ground floor (with no portcullis) or, as in earlier times, at the first floor.

These older features have curious points of similarity with the Norman keeps, but it would be a mistake to interpret

VII *The Keep, Vincennes*

them as a survival of the Romanesque. These forts were little more than watch-towers; none had a ditch round it; none of their walls is more than 5 feet thick, and there is no portcullis at the gate. It is more than likely that their rough-and-ready design was due, above all, to considerations of economy.

In spite of their somewhat archaic appearance they have one novel feature which has not been met with in the French castles examined so far. On both sides of the frontier – at Tauzia, for example, on the English side and at La Gardère on the Armagnac side – the arrow-loops, instead of having only a vertical slit, are cruciform, the horizontal slit being intended to widen the field of fire. This seems to have been an English invention; Mr. Sidney Toy (pp. 115–16) certainly refers to a number of arrow-loops of this kind in certain English fortresses from the end of the twelfth century, notably at Trematon.

The rebuilding of Blanquefort, near Bordeaux, was of the same period as the forts described above. Blanquefort belonged to the King of England, who gave it on June 16th, 1308, to Bertrand de Goth, a nephew of Pope Clement V. It will be seen later that Clement V and his cardinals built several castles in that area. But Blanquefort does not appear on the list of castles given in the *Chronique bourdeloise* of Gabriel de Lurbe (fol. 25); and from an archaeological standpoint it is also very different from the others. It is difficult, therefore, to attribute its construction to Bertrand de Goth. Léo Drouyn suggests that it was built by Edward I (1272–1307); and this is quite feasible. Before coming to the throne, Edward was Duke of Guienne and therefore he spent some time at Bordeaux; he also went back there on occasion after becoming King. Gabriel de Lurbe's *Chronique* relates that in 1287 he came to Bordeaux and spent a few days at the castle of Blanquefort; which would justify the assumption that it was rebuilt at about that time.

The castle stands on level ground in flat, marshy country. Rectangular in plan, it has no keep, but its four walls are flanked by six heavy round towers. The ground floor of each tower has either barrel or dome vaulting; the upper floors have pointed vaulting; but it is thought that between the two there was at some time an intermediate floor – which was

VIII *Le Plessis-Bourré*   E

merely boarded. (It will be remembered that only three of the five floors of the Talbot Tower at Falaise had vaulted ceilings.)

The outstanding features of Blanquefort, however, are the defence arrangements at the top of the castle. All the towers are ringed with hoards, of which the beams and their ties are mounted on double rows of corbels. These towers, like those of Ambleny, stand very close together and are linked by large arched machicolations similar to those at Niort but with pointed instead of round arches. The towers themselves are no higher than the curtains: the crests of the towers and walls are therefore all on one level and form a broad, paved wall-walk completely free of any obstacle throughout the whole perimeter of the castle. This is an improvement on the continuous wall-walk already described at Yèvre-le-Châtel – dating from the beginning of the century – where a similar result was obtained by greatly increasing the height of the curtains. This terraced roof at Blanquefort was unique among French castles at the time, but a rather earlier one existed in the Kingdom of the Two Sicilies at Castel del Monte in Cipulia, built by the Emperor Frederick III in the middle of the thirteenth century. It is not by any means unlikely that the English king had some knowledge of this famous castle; but this is pure conjecture.

Apart from the English castles, however, a number of foreign castles were built in Guienne at the beginning of the fourteenth century as a result of purely fortuitous circumstances.

Clement V, the first of the Avignon Popes, was a native of Villandraut (Gironde), in the diocese of Bazas. The castle he built there during his pontificate (1305–14) is the most perfect example of the Phillip-Augustus formula to be seen today.

The castle stands in flat country and is of rectangular plan with outside measurements of 170 feet by 140 feet. It is surrounded by wide moats and has four strongly projecting corner towers in addition to two towers guarding the gate. There is no keep. As would be expected, the towers are circular; the walls are 87 feet high, 19 feet thick and battered at the base. Each tower has four floors; the lowest room, which

is in the thickness of the battered plinth, has barrel vaulting
and no means of exit or entry except through a hole in the
crown of the vaulting. The ground- and the first-floor rooms
have eight-panelled pointed vaulting; there is no vaulting on
the second floor; communication between the floors (excluding the basement) is by a spiral staircase in the thickness of
the walls. The crest of the curtains is level with the second
floor of the towers, which at that point have a passage cut
through them so that the wall-walk is unobstructed throughout its length. The arrow-loops (which are 'staggered') are
cruciform like those of the Gascony forts; a complete row of
them encircles the castle at ground-level. Following Phillip-
Augustus's formula there is no stone machicolation; all the
towers and curtains were surmounted with hoards, indicated
by the presence of a few put-log holes still visible in the tower
on the left of the gate and on the east and west curtains. The
numerous brattices on all the floors in the deep corners
between the towers and the curtains were used as latrines.
On the face where the gate stands these brattices are con-
cealed in a lightly-built stone shelter. Access to the castle
was by means of a footbridge resting on two rough stone
plinths on each side of the moat. A passage 16 feet long led
from the gate to the inner courtyard. It is flanked externally
by two towers and defended internally by a number of
devices: one portcullis, three fall-traps, two doors, and arrow-
loops in the walls on either side. Built against the towers in
front of the outer door was a small barbican with its own
gate, the hinges of which can still be seen.

Except on the side where the gateway stands, the courtyard
is surrounded by living quarters which, judging by the
vestiges still remaining, must have been on a lavish scale.
Some elegant tracery is still visible on the windows of the
first floor looking out on to the courtyard or on to the outside
walls; there are also carved bosses in the vaulting of the
towers, of which the best known is on the first floor of the
south-west tower; it represents the Pope himself, seated,
bearded and crowned, holding his crozier in the left hand
and giving his blessing with the right.

In the commune of Mazères, about ten miles from Villandraut, is the castle of Roquetaillade, built by Cardinal

Gaillard de la Mote, a nephew of Clement V. According to Gabriel de Lurbe's *Chronique* (fol. 5) it is contemporary with Villandraut, of which it is, in fact, a faithful copy on a reduced scale, its outside measurements being 108 feet by 75 feet, compared with 170 feet by 140 feet at Villandraut. Roquetaillade has the same quadrilateral plan, with four corner towers and two towers guarding the gate; the same battered walls, continuous wall-walk and cruciform arrow-loops. It differs, however, from Villandraut in having a central square keep incorporated into the domestic buildings of the courtyard, thereby greatly restricting their size. The keep also prevents any of their rooms from opening on to the courtyard, with the result that a number of windows had to be made in the outer walls of the first floor in order to give light to the living quarters. As a measure of protection against escalade, each of these windows is surmounted by a brattice. At some later date these brattices were ludicrously restored (even to the point of embellishing them with pinnacles), but their existence prior to the restoration is proved by the Léo Drouyn etchings of 1859 and 1862 and by the evidence given in his book, *La Guienne militaire*. These brattices are one of the most interesting features of Roque-taillade. Unlike Najac, where they were considered as a special organ of defence for exceptional use only, the brattices at Roquetaillade are used systematically and in large numbers in many parts of the building, although not in all. The towers, for instance, are equipped with hoards and the curtains with the more efficient stone machicolations; but at Blanquefort – where precisely the same policy was followed – the arched machicolations seem almost antiquated compared with the brattices at Roquetaillade, which must be amongst the first of their kind to be used in France. Slightly earlier examples, however, are to be seen in the ramparts at Aigues-Mortes; those of the Krac des Chevaliers are, of course, far older than either.

In addition to Villandraut and Roquetaillade, Gabriel de Lurbe's *Chronique bourdeloise* (fol. 25) mentions five other castles as having been built in the same district during the pontificate of Clement V 'either by him or by his attendant cardinals'. Of these the best-known is La Brède (see Plate IV)

famous as the home of Montesquieu on the eighteenth
century. But Gabriel de Lurbe's statement should not be
allowed to go unchallenged.

During the thirteenth and fourteenth centuries La Brède
belonged to the La Lande family, represented at the time of
Clement V by Gaillard de la Lande – whose will is dated
April 5th, 1313 – and by his son Arnaud, who succeeded
him. So far as we know, no cardinal had any hand in
building the castle, which was already in existence before
Clement V's reign (1305–14). The Gascony Rolls (Bémont
edition, No. 859) refer to an order by Edward I dated
June 4th, 1285, calling for an inquiry into a complaint laid
by Gaillard de la Lande that his fortified residence had
been sacked and destroyed by the Provost of the Isle-Saint-
Georges. It is highly probable (and this is supported by the
Chronique bourdeloise) that the castle was rebuilt soon after.
Some additions and alterations were evidently made later
however, for Abbé Baurein in his *Variétés bordelaises* (v. 36)
mentions that the archives of La Brède contain letters patent
dated 1419 authorising Jean de La Lande to fortify his
home.[1]

La Brède has certainly none of the general characteristics
of a castle either of the early fourteenth or early fifteenth
century. The building, which is surrounded by a wide moat,
is roughly polygonal with a number of faces of varying shape
and size. The only flanking defence is from a circular tower
against the west side. The impression it gives is of a curtain
wall rebuilt on earlier foundations round an old Norman
keep. The fourteenth- and fifteenth-century addition must be
the tower 100 feet high on the west side. Assuming that the
series of machicolations surmounting it were part of the
original construction, this tower could not date back to the
fourteenth century; it must have formed part of the fortification authorised in 1419. If, on the contrary, the machicolations
were added later, the tower itself must have been built at
the beginning of the fourteenth century.

Villandraut, however, was merely a private residence. Once

---

[1] The 'Notes on the Parish of La Brède in *Variétés bordelaises* were written by Latapieè;
the judge of La Brède, who was a friend of the Montesquieu family.

it had become evident that Avignon was to be the permanent seat of Papal authority, the desire arose for it to be established there on a scale in keeping with its high office.

Pope John XXII (1316–34) had taken up residence in the bishop's palace and had had considerable improvements made to it. Later, Benedict XII (1334–42), who was a Cistercian monk, carried out a complete restoration of the building, adding close by the massive Pope's Tower and its annexes for use respectively as an abbatial house and as private apartments.

The new residence, austere in style and entirely bare of ornamental carving, was in reality a fortress, with walls surmounted by wide, pointed-arch machicolations. It is a mistake to assume that these machicolations were added later or were a particular feature of southern France. They were in common use at that time throughout the country – and perhaps the only type in use, as witness the castle of Farcheville (Seine-et-Oise), which the historian Dom Fleureau of Étampes dates from 1291, or the castle of La Grange-Bléneau (Seine-et-Marne), built in the early fourteenth century.

A much more intriguing form of machicolation is found, however, on the two square towers: La Campane (rebuilt by Benedict XII in 1339–40), and Trouillas (completed by Clement VI in 1346). M. Paul Deschamps (*Crac des Chevaliers*, pp. 265–66) refers to similar machicolations dating from 1271 and 1285 on the Krac des Chevaliers; these were added by the Mohammedans immediately after their capture of the fortress. It is extremely difficult to say when this method of defence was first introduced into the West. To the best of our knowledge the machicolations on the castle of the Popes can be definitely considered as before their time and are particularly interesting on this account. It would be quite wrong to claim that they were copies from the near-by fortifications at Villeneuve-lès-Avignon, which are definitely of later date; the Saint André fort and the upper part of the Philippe-le-Bel Tower date only from the reign of Jean le Bon (1350–64).

Benedict XII's successor was Clement VI (1342–52), a great Prince of the Church and former Chancellor of France, who almost doubled the area covered by the pontifical palace

IX *Chambord, The North Façade*

and added two wings on the south side – the 'opus novum' –
enclosing the great courtyard known as the Place du Palais.
From outside, the 'opus novum', with its walls surmounted
by arched machicolations, preserves its fortress-like character.
But in sharp contrast to the austerity of Benedict XII's
castle, the interior decoration of the new wings betrays an
evident desire for refinement and luxury. Jean de Loubières,
the master-builder from Tarascon, built for Clement VI a
palace in the Flamboyant Gothic style. Its outstanding
feature is the south wing, which comprises two vast superimposed structures each 170 feet long and 50 feet wide. On
the ground floor is the Grande Audience (or Grand Council
Chamber) where only the most important cases were heard,
with its double aisles separated by a row of five pillars embellished with colonnettes; on the floor above is the Clementine
Chapel with the single nave typical of the churches of
southern France.

The lavish use of pointed vaulting in the 'opus novum' shows
that Jean de Loubières had learnt much from the architects
of northern France; but the new palace also clearly shows the
influence of ultramontane ideas.

The grand staircase in the south wing, has, admittedly,
pointed vaulting, but its two straight flights separated by a
string-wall are entirely in the Italian tradition.

The Italian influence is even more noticeable in the
painted interior decoration. A few mural paintings had been
executed during Benoit XII's reign; one of them, a large
foliated design in red on a blue background, is still to be seen
in the Pope's bedchamber; its effect is undoubtedly striking
but it is purely ornamental and impersonal. Clement VI,
on the contrary, conceived a plan of his own which, by its
sheer splendour, would enhance the brilliance of the pontifical authority. He decided to decorate every room in the
palace with works of art portraying figures; and with this
object he enlisted the services of a number of Italian painters.
What followed in Avignon was destined to be repeated two
centuries later at Fontainebleau: a team of many artists
went to work covering the walls of the palace with their
paintings. At Avignon the work was directed by Matteo de
Giovanetti of Viterbo; some of the artists came from beyond

the Alps, some from the cisalpine territories: Dominique de Boulbonne, Robin de Romans, Barthélémy de Marseilles and others.

A few fragments of their work – mainly paintings of religious subjects – have survived: the 'Life of Saint Martial', painted in 1344 and 1345 in the oratory on the first floor of the small Saint John Tower, the 'Lives of Saints John the Baptist and John the Evangelist', in process of painting during 1347 in the oratory on the ground floor of the same tower, and 'The Prophets' painted about 1353, on one of the panels of the vaulting of the Grand Council Chamber.

On the other hand, the style of decoration in the room known as the 'Chambre du Cerf' (adjacent to and communicating with the Pope's Bedchamber) is entirely secular. This room is in the small Wardrobe Tower erected by Clement VI, immediately after his accession to the Papal throne, in order to enlarge the private apartments. The paintings in it are of hunting and fishing scenes, of children playing in an orchard planted almost entirely with Mediterranean shrubs and trees: orange, pomegranate, fig, mulberry, oleander, and umbrella pine. These paintings are in sharp contrast to the other murals in the palace, not only in their subject but even more in the realism of their style, which is surprisingly modern in a 1343 context. Efforts have been made to identify the author or the authors of this remarkably original composition. The financial accounts relating to the paintings in the Wardrobe Tower are still preserved in the archives of the Vatican; but they are so inexplicit – owing to the participation of both French and Italian artists – that they lend themselves to a variety of interpretations. Mrs. Betty Kurth wrote in 1912, 'The style of the murals excludes them from being of Italian workmanship'. Mlle Marguerite Rogues agrees with Mrs. Kurth and attributes these paintings to Robin de Romans, saying (in the *Bulletin monumental*, 1960) 'This is an entirely French treatment of the Franco-Flemish tapestries'. Honoré Lalande, however, considers that 'the style and technique of the figures are entirely Italian'. Robert André-Michel is less categorical; he emphasises the international atmosphere at Avignon and he concludes: 'One is tempted to say that at Avignon the naturalistic school of painting, which was to win such universal acclaim later, derived its *matter* from France and its *form* from Italy. France drew upon her greater cultural refinement, her wealth, and her instinct for elegance; Italy drew upon the superb technique of her artists.'

5 | The Hundred Years War
The return to the Norman formula

Just at the time when Clement VI was completing his task of making the Palace of the Popes into what Froissart described as 'the finest and strongest building in the world', war broke out once more between France and England. A series of disasters followed for France. She was defeated at Crécy (1346) and Poitiers (1356); there were riots in Paris; the quickly-crushed peasants' revolt ('La Jacquerie') in Beauvaisis. For many years bands of brigands terrorised the countryside. The final tragedy came in 1392 with the madness of King Charles VI and the outbreak of civil war. During the long period of peace which had preceded hostilities, castles had been allowed to fall into disrepair. It now became necessary to put them into working order or build new ones; with the result that the Hundred Years War was a period of great activity in all forms of military construction.

One of the most noticeable signs of this renewed activity was the appearance of machicolated galleries supported on consoles. These galleries became a permanent feature at the top of all walls and towers from that time onwards. Many old keeps were brought up to date by surmounting them with machicolations of this kind; the Philippe-le-Bel Tower at Villeneuve-lès-Avignon, already mentioned; Pouzauges in Poitou, Lavardin in Touraine, Chambois in Normandy, Montlhéry near Paris and many others all over France.

A number of changes are noticeable over the years in the types of machicolation supported on consoles. On the ramparts at Avignon for example, in the middle of the fourteenth century, the corbels were spanned by small arches. These earliest types developed later – in the last quarter of the

fourteenth century – into those at Méhun-sur-Yèvre (Cher)
or Largoët-en-Elven (Morbihan), for example, where the
arches are pointed trefoil. At the Solidor Tower at Saint
Servan, however, the arch had already been replaced – prior
to 1371 – by a plain lintel, and these lintels became estab-
lised practice during the fifteenth century. The lintels at
Tarascon, built in the second quarter of the century, were
quite bare; but later types were decorated with increasingly
ornate rows of blind arches. At Ussé (Indre-et-Loire), it is
possible to trace the history of the building from the various
types of arches used. In castles in Brittany the consoles carrying the machicolation took the novel form of an inverted
pyramid. Roger Grand, in the *Bulletin monumental*, 1952,
p. 41, reports an example of these 'Breton machicolations' on
the keep at Largoët-en-Elven in the last quarter of the fourteenth century. They became general later throughout the
province: at Sucinio (Morbihan), at Tonquédec (Côtes-du-
Nord), at Combourg (Ille-et-Vilaine) and elsewhere. Isolated
examples are found later still in various parts of the kingdom:
at Bonaguil (Lot-et-Garonne) at the end of the fifteenth
century, on the Marques Tower at Chenonceaux (Indre-et-
Loire) between 1513 and 1514, at La Rochefoucauld (Cha-
rente) about 1530 and at Chaumont (Loir-et-Cher) in the
third quarter of the sixteenth century.

The hinged drawbridge was another special feature introduced at about this time. The far end of the bridge was
attached – by ropes or chains – to two long beams or shafts
having counterbalances on their inner ends. When the bridge
is raised they swing on central pivots and fit into vertical
recesses in the sides of the walls. This type of drawbridge was
not yet in use on the gate of the Saint-André fort at Villeneuve-lès-Avignon, which dates – according to M. Fernand
Benoit – from the reign of John II,[1] but it is found at Vincennes, built later by Charles V.

In general, the castles built at this time showed less and
less affinity with the thirteenth-century type as exemplified by
Villandraut; and eventually the Phillip-Augustus formula
was abandoned altogether. The change seems to have begun

[1] 'Jean le Bon'. 1319–64.

in the castles built by the Crown: the Louvre, the Bastille
and Vincennes.

The rebuilding of the Louvre and the erection of the
Bastille were both part of a general plan to rebuild entirely
the city walls of Paris. This plan had been hastily drawn up
by Etienne Marcel immediately after the battle of Poitiers
(1356), but it was taken in hand more thoroughly later
by Charles V.

The new walls, which joined the Seine at the level of the
present entrance to the Place du Carrousel, brought the
Louvre within the city precincts and thereby completely
destroyed its military value. This explains the fact that the
work undertaken by the new king (1364) transformed the
Louvre, as built by Phillip-Augustus, from a fortress into a
residential palace. A new storey with wide casement windows
was added; the towers were surmounted by machicolated
wall-walks; living quarters were built on the top of the
building, and the roofs were embellished with weathercocks
and gilded finials. The interior courtyard was enriched by a
magnificent spiral staircase supported on pillars bearing
statues of the royal family.

It seems certain that when Jean, duc de Berry, brother
of Charles V, built his castles at Méhun-sur-Yèvre and
Saumur he was strongly influenced by the style of the new
work at the Louvre. Méhun-sur-Yèvre was, in fact, the work
of the master-builder, Guy de Dammartin, who had been
employed at the Louvre. From two miniatures in the
Chantilly Book of Hours we learn more about these two
castles than from what remains of them today. They were of
the traditional rectangular plan with corner towers; there
was no keep at Saumur; at Méhun one of the towers was
stronger than the other three; the battered bases of the walls
and the few openings at the lower levels were also in the
tradition. What was new (and a complete departure from the
Phillip-Augustus formula) was the unusual height of the
walls, the galleries of machicolations round them, and, above
all, high up above the wall-walk, the magnificently appointed
living quarters. It should be added that at Saumur the towers,
which were circular up to about half their height, were made
octagonal above that point and supported by buttresses.

The most important of all the strong points along the new wall built by Charles V round Paris was the Bastille, which guarded the Saint Antony Gate. It was built between 1370 and 1382 as a massive fortress on the polygonal plan, with eight circular towers of equal strength; the walls were battered and their bases had very few loopholes. Its unusual features were the raising of the height of the curtains up to that of the towers, and the continuous wall-walk round the whole perimeter of the building. A similar arrangement has already been observed at Blanquefort, where, however, hoards are used alternately with arched machicolation along the wall-walk. At the Bastille, however, the wall-walk was an uninterrupted gallery, entirely made up of machicolations mounted on consoles, which followed the winding contour round the whole building.

This arrangement gave considerably increased mobility to the garrison and was copied, during the fifteenth century, in many castles in various parts of France: at La Ferté-Milon (Aisne) prior to the assassination of Louis of Orleans in 1407; at Tonquédec (Côtes du Nord) which was rebuilt some time after 1407; at Tarascon (Bouches du Rhône) built mainly during the second quarter of the fifteenth century (see Plate IV); then (later) under Louis XI, at the royal castle of Langeais (Indre-et-Loire) and Rambures (Somme); finally at Ussé (Indre-et-Loire) under either Charles VIII or Louis XII. The purely ornamental wall-walk built on to Chaumont by Diane de Poitiers in the third quarter of the sixteenth century followed the same plan.

It was Vincennes, however, that represented the final and complete break with the Phillip-Augustus formula. Ever since the twelfth century the Crown had owned a manor there together with a large hunting park. The present castle was originally no more than a keep; it bore an inscription (destroyed in 1791) setting out the various dates at which it was built or rebuilt. The foundations were laid by Phillip VI in 1337, but building operations were interrupted by the war with England. John II resumed the work between 1361 and 1364 on his return from captivity, erecting the first three floors of the tower. Charles V completed the building in 1370. (See Plate VII and p. 79.)

The keep is a massive structure 170 feet high and 54 feet square. Its walls are 10 feet thick at the base and are flanked by four circular towers. It seems to have been modelled on the great tower of the Temple, to which it bears a striking resemblance. (The towers of the Louvre and of the Temple were the strongest in Paris.) Vincennes has the same general plan as the Temple; the vaulting on all the floors is also the same: four panels of pointed vaulting supported on a central pillar. The difference in the dates of the two buildings, however, is clearly indicated by the fact that the gallery of machicolations surmounting Vincennes is of a quite new type; it is merely a parapet with holes cut through it. The topmost floor, which was originally crenellated, is set back from the line of the main walls so as to command the wall-walk if it were occupied by the enemy. This is probably the first example of an arrangement of this kind. The chemise surrounding the tower has deeply battered bases to the walls and is surmounted by a gallery of machicolations mounted on consoles; the moat around it was over 70 feet wide, but it has been partly filled in since.

We do not know what Phillip VI had in mind when he laid the foundations of the keep; but it is quite clear that when John II was building the three lower floors of this great tower his intention was to make a royal abode. The ornamental carving on all the central pillars and on the shafts supporting the vaulting is very delicate and highly skilled; and in the larger rooms an almost unique degree of refinement is achieved by panelling the vaulting with wood in order to diminish the cold effect of the stone. This reversion to the older Norman conception of the castle may appear surprising at first sight; but it becomes easily comprehensible when it is remembered that three years before, while the King was still in captivity, Etienne Marcel had invaded the palace and had had the marshals massacred in the Dauphin's own room and under the Dauphin's own eyes. This anxiety for protection against a possible invasion of the castle by the populace is indicated by a curious – and somewhat archaic – addition made (according to Captain de Fossa) by Charles V. The door of the royal apartments was on the first floor of the keep. Access to it was by a stairway built into the gatehouse

guarding the entrance to the chemise; and this stairway led
first to a footbridge and thence to a drawbridge fitting into
grooves which are still visible on the eastern face of the tower.[1]

Vincennes was Charles V's favourite residence. Christine
de Pisan records that the King often expressed the wish to
have 'his dearest friends living in fine manor houses' close
to the castle. These buildings, together with Saint Louis's
own manor house, which was still standing, and the Sainte
Chapelle (begun in 1379 and finished only in 1552) were
finally enclosed in a vast bailey surrounded by a curtain wall
measuring 370 yards by 202 yards, which had been begun
before the keep itself was finished and was in active progress
in 1373.

The planning of this *enceinte* marks the ultimate break with
the Phillip-Augustus tradition. The ditches surrounding the
curtains are as wide as those round the keep. The curtains
themselves are rather below the usual height and are flanked
by nine towers rising to 90 feet above them. They are deeply
battered at the base and are surmounted by galleries of
machicolations mounted on consoles. Only one of the towers
has kept its original height, the eight others having been cut
down during the nineteenth century to the level of the top of
the curtains. Like the old Norman keeps the towers were
rectangular in plan and strongly buttressed. They had vaulting on the ground and on the top floors, this being necessary
to support a platform intended for spring-propelled artillery.
Each tower represented an autonomous defence system
capable of working in isolation; and here once again we see
a return to the concepts of the twelfth century; at the castle
of Saone in Syria, many of the towers built by the Crusaders
in the twelfth century were in fact small forts capable of acting
as independent units of defence.

As we shall see later, the general plan of Vincennes served
as a model for Chambord in the sixteenth century. In the
fourteenth century, however, it was not the bailey-wall but

---

[1] The wall-walk makes a detour round a rectangular latrine-tower, built on to the north-
west turret of the keep. Captain de Fossa is inclined to consider this auxiliary tower as of
military significance – although he seems unable to explain it. We think that it is sited in
this way for mere reasons of convenience, that is, to isolate the latrines as much as possible.
This tower did not prejudice the flanking of the north face of the keep because its ventilating
loopholes could if necessary be used as arrow-loops.

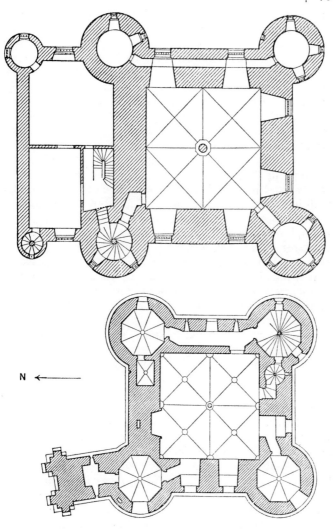

N ←————————

FIG. 3 (*above*) TOWER OF THE TEMPLE (PARIS). *Plan drawn by Bourla, architect, 1793.* (*below*) THE KEEP, VINCENNES. *Plan by P. Varin*

[From the archives of the Commission of Historic Monuments, new entries, 1908, No. 13149]

the keep which was being copied by others. When Jean de Berry, brother to Charles V, rebuilt the great tower – the Maubergeon Tower – of his palace of Poitiers between 1384–86, his master-builder, Guy de Dammartin, who had worked on the Louvre, copied the keep of Vincennes, using the same quadrilateral plan with round towers at the corners, the same pointed vaulting on every floor; the only difference being that the ribs of the vaulting in the large rooms were not supported on a central pillar but on a row of three pillars which divide the rooms into two parallel aisles.

The influence of the Maubergeon Tower made itself felt not only in Poitou but also in Berry and Auvergne, which were part of Jean de Berry's domain. The quadrilateral plan with its round towers was adopted in several private castles so small that they were little more than single towers; as for example, Romefort (Indre), Alleuze (Cantal) – both built at about 1411 – and Anjony (Cantal), built in 1435. The castle at Vals (Cantal) belongs to the same group except that it has six instead of four towers, one of which is solid and serves as a buttress. (See outside cover.) It is impossible to say whether the large number of castles built during the Hundred Years War was due merely to the influence of Vincennes or to the need for greater security in troublous times. What these castles clearly show, however, is the great variety of the plans adopted by their builders; as great indeed, as in those of the twelfth-century keeps. Thanks to Roger Grand's researches, Brittany provides a number of examples. The traditional cylindrical tower is found at Cesson, near Saint Brieuc, built by Jean IV, duc de Bretagne. This tower was certainly in existence in 1388 because its governor was appointed in that year. Tonquédec – rebuilt in 1407 – also has a cylindrical tower. At Largoët-en-Elven and at Oudon, however, the octagonal plan was followed. According to Roger Grand, the massive keep at Largoët-en-Elven was built by the Malestroit family – Jean II and his brother Alain – some time between 1375 and 1380; the authority to build Oudon was granted on May 22nd, 1392. The Solidor Tower at Saint-Servan, which was already standing in 1371 (*Bulletin monumental*, 1951, p. 358), is extremely unusual in that it takes the form of a triangular prism with a powerful

x *Bonaguil*

circular tower at each corner. Note that the entrances at Cesson and Tonquédec are placed – as at Vincennes – at the level of the first or even the second floor. The small castle of Brugnac (Gironde) was built some fifty or seventy-five years earlier in what was then the English part of Guienne. In certain particulars it resembles the Gascony forts of the late thirteenth century. Brugnac was a square keep with oblique corner buttresses; the two entrances were sited one exactly above the other; the first, on the lower floor (which served only as a store room and had no communication with the rest of the building) was 6 feet above ground level; the main entrance was on a level with the first floor. Some time later, about 1400, a staircase turret was built 6 feet in front of the façade where the two entrances are sited; footbridges led from it to each of the two doors. This arrangement seems to have been copied from a similar one already described at Vincennes.

The frequent recurrence of outdated systems in the castles we have been describing has led Enlart (p. 577) to refer to what he calls a 'persistence of the Norman type of castle'. But this remark seems hardly appropriate to the situation in France at that time, since there was no real continuity in the development of castle-building; a gap of a century and a half separates the Norman keeps from those built during the Hundred Years War. We think it would be more accurate to say that after a long period of inactivity the fourteenth and fifteenth centuries marked a curious revival of a number of Norman concepts; but this revival in no way prevented the castles built during the Hundred Years War from adopting new ideas, such as machicolations mounted on consoles, and hinged drawbridges. (Brugnac, it is true, is an exception to this rule, but it should be remembered that it was on English territory).

Apart from small buildings which were little more than keeps, very few completely new castles were being built at this time. Two must be mentioned, however: Pierrefonds and La Ferté-Milon, both built by Louis d'Orleans (brother of Charles VI) between 1392, when Louis inherited his apanage of Valois, and November 23rd, 1407, which was the date of his death. In both these castles the influence of Vincennes is apparent from the way in which the residential quarters have been fitted into a square keep. But the wall enclosing the keep is far smaller than that of Vincennes, and has no points of similarity with it. At Pierrefonds the wall-walk encircles the whole fortress and is commanded by an upper floor set back from the outer walls. But whereas the upper floor at Vincennes exists only on the towers, at Pierrefonds it also exists on the curtains and it therefore commands the wall-walk throughout its length. (See Plate XXXVII.) The castle of La Ferté-Milon was never finished. Only the keep and the western face of the curtain wall were completed. Two interesting features should be noted: the wall-walk is continuous – as at the Bastille – along the towers and curtains; and the towers themselves are prow-shaped like those already observed in the keeps of La Roche-Guyon, Issoudun and Château-Gaillard. This type of tower dates back to the Norman period, but it was still in use during the thirteenth century; the southern face of the curtain wall at Loches and the Narbonne Gate at Carcassonne are well-known examples.

The sophisticated tastes of fourteenth-century society naturally found expression in the castles of the period, which admittedly were fortified places; but their appearance makes it immediately clear that they were also lordly residences. The lavish style of the upper parts of the Louvre, of Méhun-sur-Yèvre and of Saumur has already been mentioned. Even below the level of the wall-walk the façades of the castle were often embellished with ornamental carving. The picture of the Louvre in the 'Très riches heures' at Chantilly shows a statue against one of the towers guarding the southern gate. At Pierrefonds and at La Ferté-Milon the towers were ornamented with statues of knights and ladies standing in finely-carved niches. The Maubergeon Tower at Poitiers is ringed with a group of fourteen figures in civilian costume – which may be Counts of Poitou. The entrance at La Ferté-Milon is decorated with a very fine bas-relief depicting the Coronation of the Virgin, and on the south curtain at Pierrefonds there was a similar carving of the Annunciation.

The principal rooms inside the building were the private apartments – consisting of the bedroom and its annexes – and the great hall, which was the official reception-room.

The delicacy of the sculptures at Vincennes is an indication
of the lavish care bestowed upon the decorations of the royal
apartments. At Poitiers, on the other hand, is an excellent
example – in a remarkably good state of preservation – of
the great hall. The greater part of this huge room dates back
to the Plantagenets, that is, to the end of the twelfth century.
The exaggeratedly slender columns supporting the arches
are typical of the Angevine Gothic style. But about 1390,
Jean de Berry completely rebuilt the southern wall of the
room, covering it almost completely with an immense triple
fireplace surmounted by open canopies carved with all the
extravagance of the Flamboyant Gothic. Above them are
four statues said to represent Charles VI and Isabel of
Bavaria, and Jean de Berry with Jeanne de Boulogne, the
last of his wives.

6 | The last of the Fortified Castles
The Grand Style in Architecture

The early years of the fifteenth century were amongst the most
tragic in the history of France. On October 25th, 1415, the
flower of French chivalry were slaughtered at Agincourt; the
dynasty and even the independence of the whole kingdom
were in grave danger. The building of castles was halted for a
time. When it revived – towards the middle of the fifteenth
century – the austerity of the new castles contrasted sharply
with the lavish style of the old.

On his return from 25 years' captivity Charles d'Orléans –
whose father had built Pierrefonds and La Ferté-Milon
– carried out extensive alterations to his castle at Blois.
Part of the gallery he then built is still in existence. The
building itself is unpretentious and has little sculptured
ornamentation; but its fine proportions and the happy
blending of brick and stone give it elegance and charm.

Style in architecture remained austere, however, throughout Louis XI's reign; the famous stone-and-brick manor
house of Plessis-lès-Tours is typical of the period. Note,
however, that the highly carved façade that appears in a
drawing of the castle in the Gaignières collections was not

the work of Louis XI; it dates only from the time of Louis XII and Francis I.

It was during the second half of the fifteenth century that the last of the fortified castles were built. From then onwards military engineers had to adapt their plans to the increasing use of artillery which, as a result of the work of Charles VII's Master Gunner, Jean Bureau, and his brother Gaspard, had made considerable progress during the Hundred Years War.

Langeais (Indre-et-Loire) was built in 1465 or thereabouts by order of Louis XI, under the supervision of one of his trusted lieutenants, Jean Bourré. It is a grim-looking fortress which has two particular features characteristic of the castles of Charles VII: a continuous wall-walk some 430 feet long, and an upper storey set back so as to command the wall-walk at the top of the towers. Its only novelty is a crenellated platform built on a rampart at the foot of the walls on the southern side, its object being to permit horizontal fire. It is a significant fact that Langeais was never completed; its high walls surmounted by machicolations show that it was principally designed against the danger of escalade and was therefore considered obsolete even before it was finished.

Plessis-Bourré, however, embodied much more advanced ideas. It must have been nearing completion on January 14th, 1472, for it was on that date that a contract was signed for glazing the windows of the main residential building. Like Langeais, Plessis-Bourré was the work of Jean Bourré and was of the same period. Its defence system, however, was based on the quite different policy of preventing an enemy from reaching the immediate approaches to the castle. With this object in view, the vast rectangular structure with four corner-towers was completely surrounded by an unusually wide moat with a *fausse-braie*,[1] along its inner bank. High walls being no longer a military necessity, they were used only on the rear part of the building and only to provide a number of floors for residential purposes. The remaining three wings and the two corner towers of the front wing were brought down to the height of the first floor. The need to provide for the use of new weapons is also seen in other details

---

[1] A wide, level and open platform. (See Ecouen, Plate XIV.)

XII *Carrouges, The Gate-House*

of the defence system. Holes were made in the middle of the
arrow-loops to allow the barrel of a culverin to pass through
them. Machicolations of the traditional type were only used
on the great tower on the south-east corner, which serves as a
keep. The corbel-mounted type of machicolation on the
adjoining curtain was evidently considered too vulnerable
and was replaced by a series of long vertical gulleys cut into
the wall to guide projectiles launched from above on to the
heads of attackers. The only other example of this device, so
far as we know, is at L'Isle Savary (Indre). (See Plate VIII.)

The general plan adopted at Plessis-Bourré constitutes a
new formula for the fortified castle. From the purely military
point of view, however, the formula used there was perhaps
not greatly superior to that of Langeais. Its principal advantage was that it provided for spacious residential quarters
open to the light and to the air by reason of the lower buildings
around it; and this arrangement was perfectly adaptable
to the new living conditions that arose a few years later, when
castles ceased to be fortresses and were used purely for residential purposes. During the last years of the century this
same plan was followed by Marshal de Gié for the forecourt
of his palatial residence, Le Verger (since destroyed); it was
also the model for Bury, near Blois, built between 1515–20 and
destroyed since. In the course of time it was generally
accepted as the basic plan of the typical great country house
of the sixteenth and early seventeenth centuries. It is found
even in the 'small' Versailles built by Louis XIII between
1631 and 1634. Its basic characteristic is that the forecourt
is enclosed by a low wing, or by a plain wall, or even by a
row of arches. One is fully justified, therefore, in claiming that
Plessis-Bourré was a most important landmark in the history
of great houses; it was the link between the fortified castles
of the Middle Ages and the châteaux of modern times.

It was not long before the new ideas created by Jean
Bourré began to evolve into other forms. In due course
machicolation disappeared completely and battlements were
replaced by broad chamfered parapets; loopholes were no
longer just modified types of arrow-loops; they were embrasures for guns, and they consisted of a round hole surmounted by a vertical slit for aiming purposes. The west

XIII *Blois, Courtyard Façade of the Francis I Wing*

wing of Tonquédec gives an excellent illustration of the progress made in this direction. (This wing was built with funds raised as the result of a tax levied by virtue of an authority given on November 19th, 1473.) It differs from the rest of the castle by its lower height, by the absence of machicolations and by the design of the gun embrasures.

These contrasting features are easily explained by the interval of three-quarters of a century that elapsed between the building of the older parts and the new wing of Tonquédec. A very different situation arises, however, at Bonaguil (Lot-et-Garonne). Canon Marboutin (*Congrès archéologique* 1937) makes it quite clear that Bonaguil was built in several stages; but the lapse of time between each stage was short, and it is interesting to notice how rapidly notions regarding the defence of fortified places were changing during the last years of the fifteenth century. During the third quarter of the century Jean de Roquefeuil had restored the old keep of the castle and equipped it with a gallery of machicolations; he also added a number of residential apartments. But it was his son Bringon (1482–1530) who provided it with a defence system. During the first stage (in about 1485) he dug a broad, deep ditch in front of the entrance façade of the castle; and across this ditch he threw drawbridges, which were protected by a barbican in front. He also built four corner towers on to the existing building and surmounted them with a machicolated wall-walk; and arrow-loops were cut in the walls of the towers. Up to this point, therefore, the defence system followed the traditional pattern; the second stage, which was undertaken later, brought drastic changes. Except on the front façade – where the entrance stood – the castle was completely surrounded by a low wall, which followed the contours of the ground and was pierced with embrasures to provide for horizontal gunfire. In addition, a broad platform was erected against the west side with the object of mounting large-calibre cannon that could counter the fire of any batteries sited by an enemy on the high ground facing the castle. The original defence plan at Bonaguil had been to guard against the danger of escalade; in the end, its object was to defend the place against cannon-fire. No such attack ever, in fact, took place; and one wonders how long such a castle could have held out against concentrated gunfire, which would quickly have opened breaches in the outer wall and demolished the towers of the castle itself. By the year 1500 the time of the fortified castle had passed; and Bonaguil is particularly interesting in that it represents the survival of an outdated system – the last of the French fortified castles. (See Plate x.) It is curious to note that although the warlike attributes of the medieval fortresses were of no further use in military engineering they survived for many years as features of civilian architecture. It would seem that they had come to be an indispensable part of the decoration of stately homes. It is difficult to imagine any castle of the Loire at the first quarter of the sixteenth century – Azay-le-Rideau or L'Islette or Le Lude for example – without its towers or its machicolations. And in some districts the fashion died hard; even as late as the third quarter of the century Diane de Poitiers added a machicolated wall-walk to the gateway at Chaumont, and Jacques d'Etampes made similar additions to Valençay.

The austerity of the architectural styles in vogue during the reigns of Charles VII and Louis XI seems to have persisted throughout the regency of Anne de Beaujeu. But as soon as he was freed of his sister's tutelage Charles VIII broke away from the somewhat prim traditions of his time. Already in 1493 he had put in hand the rebuilding of his castle at Amboise with the object of making it the most sumptuous residence in Europe. The work continued for six years; what remains of it today suffices to give some idea of the lavish scale of the building. All military considerations were ignored; the two huge towers flanking the north and south façades were used – as we all know – to house the great staircases. The feudal castle had become a sumptuous residence with all the lavish ornamentation of the Flamboyant Gothic, particularly in the royal apartments on the façade (much restored) overlooking the Loire, and in the famous Saint Hubert Chapel, which is carved like a jewel.

The example given by the King was quickly followed by the nobility. All the most famous châteaux of the Flamboyant Gothic style date from about 1500. Amongst them one should mention Meillant and Josselin, which were both originally fortified castles; both were greatly embellished by the addition of new interior façades.

The parts of this work still remaining at Meillant cannot be of later date than 1503, for the Order of Saint Michael, which was bestowed on the owner, Charles d'Amboise, in 1503 does not appear on the coat of arms carved over the door of the Lion Tower. The decoration is particularly rich in the upper parts of the façade, where the dormer windows are surmounted by open-work tracery and the chimneys ornamented with dummy lights and blind railings; the staircase of the Lion Tower is also embellished with blind arches, monograms and emblems.

Josselin was built by Jean de Rohan, who died in 1516. We know that work was in full progress there between 1504 and 1505. It owes the attractive originality of its façade to the magnificent two-storeyed dormer windows rising above a balustrade of varying designs, dotted here and there with crowned 'A's' – the initial of Anne de Bretagne. (See Plate xi.)

Other noblemen, although of lower rank perhaps than the Amboise or Rohan families, were equally anxious to modernise their old homes. It must suffice to mention the very attractive galleries built at Argy by Charles de Brillac, who died in 1509. The ground floor consists of elegant ogee arches and the walls are strewn with a profusion of K's and L's (the initials of Charles de Brillac and of his wife Louise) in a style of decoration which was fashionable under Charles VIII and Louis XII.

Even the sober-minded Anne of Beaujeu felt constrained to embellish her castle at Gien in about 1494. The work was done, admittedly, with an eye to economy. No costly carving or sculpture was undertaken. The ornamentation consisted entirely in a variety of designs achieved by the interplay of red and black brick and of white stone; which together give a bright note to the walls. This was not, however, an innovation at the time; a similar style had already been used at the neighbouring castle of Concressault, built by the Duc de Berry at the end of the fourteenth century; Anne de Beaujeu may well have drawn her inspiration from it.

| THE RENAISSANCE

The rebuilding of Amboise was in full swing when Charles VIII set out on his campaign against the Kingdom of Naples (1494–95). We know with what enthusiasm the French discovered Italy; we know, too, that Charles VIII brought back across the Alps twenty-two artisans 'to build and do divers works to his order and pleasure, in the Italian manner'.

Of these workmen, those who belonged to the building trades were nearly all ornamental masons, carpenters, or marquetry workers; and they made their presence felt very quickly, as witness a number of carved bosses in the vaulting of one of the great towers of Amboise.

The unexpected death of Charles VIII on April 7th, 1498, put a sudden stop to the work at Amboise; Louis XII transferred its activities to his own castle at Blois and built there the new wing which bears his name. The style, however, of this new brick-and-stone building still remained the Flamboyant Gothic. The Italian influence is only visible here and there (amongst the prevailing late Gothic) in a few exotic motifs: some foliated rosettes on the pediments of the dormer windows and on the panels of the cornice of the great staircase; and a few panels of 'grotesques' on some of the pillars of the open gallery on the ground floor.

So far as the royal buildings alone are concerned (and the 'New Rooms' at Loches confirm this) it must be admitted that up to the death of Louis XII the Italian influence in the building arts was insignificant. The new style in architecture, which we call the Renaissance, was due entirely to private initiative; and it found its expression in two forms: at Gaillon and at Nantouillet.

I | The Gaillon Formula
'The Châteaux of the Loire'

Gaillon (Eure) was the work of Louis XII's chief minister, the famous Cardinal d'Amboise, of whom Henry le Monnier wrote that he 'was, *par excellence,* the man concerned with Italian affairs'. It was in his capacity as Archbishop of Rouen that he had the castle rebuilt as a country house for the Archbishop. Building began at the end of 1501 and continued until the Cardinal's death on May 25th, 1510. It was directed at first by master-builders belonging to the Royal household, and they produced a building in the Flamboyant Gothic style ornamented here and there – as at Blois – with a number of motifs in the Italian manner. Mlle Chirol points out, however, that from 1506 onwards the Crown masons were taken away and replaced by men from Rouen, who, although perhaps of lesser repute, were more adaptable to new ideas. From that moment Gaillon began to take on an entirely new aspect, embodying the most progressive ideas of the time. The porch (which is still standing) was built between 1509 and 1510 and is one of the most interesting parts of the house because it was, in fact, the last addition made to it. The original building goes back to the archiepiscopate of Cardinal d'Estouteville in about 1460. The masons employed by Georges d'Amboise were content to rejuvenate it by altering its style of decoration.

On the more ornate Gothic façades of that time all the openings were made exactly one above the other from the ground level to the gutters, at which point a dormer window would be used to soften the harsh vertical line of the windows. In castles like Langeais or Plessis-Bourré, where the decoration was restrained, the ornamentation would be limited to crowning the windows with horseshoe dripstones; but in the more sumptuous buildings such as Meillant the windows would be framed in Gothic pilasters joined one to another from floor to floor, accentuating the vertical line of the general design.

This traditional style – which may already have existed in the building – was preserved in the porch at Gaillon. What was changed was the form of decoration, which became almost exclusively Italian. The triangular-section Gothic pilasters framing the windows were replaced by flat shafts ornamented with grotesques in bas-relief; and these shafts, like the former pilasters, were continuous from the ground floor up to the gutters. The string-course mouldings between the floors (which also exist at Meillant) were embellished with acanthus foliage, dentils and ovolos; the windows were surmounted with semicircular pediments embellished with a large shell; the dormer windows have disappeared, but from an engraving by Israel Silvestre we know that they were decorated in the same style.

By the very simple operation of replacing the Gothic by more classical ornamentation, and without changing in any way the general disposition of the façades, an apparently new architectonic formula had been created, spontaneously and, indeed, fortuitously; a formula which was destined to become famous.

Gaillon undoubtedly set a new fashion that was quickly followed. By the end of the reign of Louis XII several buildings had hastily adopted the characteristic superimposed pilasters of the Gaillon porch. Handsome staircase-towers were added, for example, to the castles at Montsoreau and Saint-Ouen-de-Chemazé. An even better example is the manor of La Possonnière, the birthplace of Ronsard in 1524, which his father had had rebuilt between 1514 and 1515. Ronsard – most famous of the Pléiade[1] – never came into possession of the house; but he made frequent references to it in his poems. Speaking of death he would use the expressions, *Il faut partir* or *avant que de partir*, which (for him) are reminiscent of the motto: *Avant Partir* repeated in many places on the walls of his home. On the window-rail (restored) and on the fireplace of the great hall are bas-reliefs depicting a burning bush – a

[1] Ronsard, Du Bellay, Remy Belleau, Jodelle, Dorat, Baïf and Pontus de Tyard.

rebus of his own name, *ronce ard*[1] – which inspired the poet to write of his love for Cassandra:

> *Je veux encor de ma pâle couleur*
> *Aux bords du Loir faire naître une fleur*
> *Qui de mon nom et de mon mal soit peinte.*

But Montsoreau, Chemazé and La Possonnière were only modest imitations of the formula embodied in the porch at Gaillon. It was after the accession of Francis I on January 1st, 1515, that the new style was to come into its own. The new monarch was twenty years old, bursting with energy, keenly interested in architecture and a passionate admirer of everything Italian. As soon as he became king he determined to impose his own ideas at Blois, which since the reign of Louis XII had become the principal residence of the Crown. One's attention is immediately gripped, as one enters the courtyard, by the startling appearance of the façade of the wing built by Francis I, entirely in stone, contrasting sharply with the more sober brick-and-stone of the older buildings. On closer inspection, however, it is clear that this façade has no essentially new feature. The windows, flanked by superimposed pilasters with flat shafts ornamented with grotesques and composite Italianate capitals, are obviously copied from the porch at Gaillon. The double rows of horizontal moulding between the floors are, however, an imitation of the adjoining wings, built by Charles d'Orléans and Louis XII; and the combination of vertical and horizontal lines has produced a general quadrilateral effect which must have seemed very original at the time, although, in fact, it embodied no specifically new idea. (See Plate XIII.)

The King was young and popular, and he had just covered himself with glory at the battle of Marignan; no wonder that his apparently new architectural style was enthusiastically adopted by all the nobility. It was characteristic of all the buildings we call the 'Châteaux of the Loire', many of them being in the Loire valley, which at that time was the favourite resort of the French Court: Azay-le-Rideau, Le Lude, Saint-Aignan, Villegongis, Bury (since disappeared), etc. But

---

[1] *Ronce* – bramble or bush. *Ard* – ardent – burning.

it should not be thought that the new style had any regional character. It was adopted throughout the country wherever the great nobles were rebuilding or remodelling their ancestral homes: by Anne de Montmorency at Chantilly in Valois; by Count François de Rochefoucauld in Angoumois; by Galiot de Genouillac at Assier in Quercy; by the King of Navarre at Pau; and by many others. The 'Châteaux of the Loire' were to be found, in fact, in every part of France.

All that was thought necessary to rejuvenate an old building was to redecorate the walls externally in the new style; this was the method used on the east façade at La Rochefoucauld amongst others. On new buildings, however, the old military features were jealously retained as being the indispensable attributes of a stately home. They were, of course, entirely artificial; the machicolations were mere ornament; the awe-inspiring towers were only a sham. Houses such as Le Lude, Apremont, Villegongis are perfect examples of what is meant by the 'Châteaux of the Loire'; they are pseudo-fortified castles with an added decoration in the Italian manner. The new style, however, had hardly been established when it began to evolve. A close study of the inner façade of Francis I's new wing at Blois is very enlightening on this point. The right-hand portion, which comprises three window-openings, is heavily ornamented in the manner of the porch at Gaillon; the windows on the first floor have double transoms; the window-casings and pilasters on the second floor (the only floor which was completed) are covered with arabesques; and the salamanders on the wall panels are framed in large lozenge mouldings. On the left-hand portion of the façade the style is more restrained; the double transoms have disappeared; the shafts of the pilasters and the window-casings are bare of ornament; the salamanders on the panels stand out unframed from the bare wall. It should be added that in both the right and left-hand sections the proportions and outline of the mouldings have been completely altered; the sharp angles and the deep shadows produced by the Gothic mouldings have disappeared, giving place to the sturdy, square-cut outlines of the Classical style.

For the most part, the new architectural style refused to be confined within the narrow limits of the Gaillon formula.

xv *Fontaine-Henri*

New – and unmistakably foreign – ideas were brought in to help in its further development. The work of Giròlamo della Robbia is of prime importance in this context and should not be overlooked. We know from the records discovered by Dr. Lesueur and M. Michelot that he arrived in France early in 1518 and was at that time employed by the Crown. It is quite possible that it was he who was responsible for curbing the somewhat heavy-handed exuberance of the Gaillon style and for initiating the masons of France into the more restrained elegance and refinement of Florentine art.

It undoubtedly found its perfect expression in the castle of Azay-le-Rideau, built between 1518 and 1527 by the financier, Gilles Berthelot. Azay-le-Rideau has much in common and is contemporary with the Francis I wing at Blois. Its dummy machicolations and corner watch-towers give it a certain military air; but these features are not emphasised and they serve merely to enliven the general appearance of the outer façades. The influence of Blois is visible everywhere – on the outside and within the courtyard – in the combination of the superimposed pilasters and in the double rows of horizontal mouldings between the floors. The style is plain, with little ornament; the shafts of the pilasters, the window casings and the wall-space between the windows are quite bare. But this sober background accentuates the sophistication of the ornamental carving (which is exceptionally fine) on the capitals, the pediments of the windows and particularly on the magnificent inner façade of the staircase, the splendour of which is enhanced by the quiet simplicity surrounding it. (See Plate vi.)

A faint echo of the medieval should be noted in the dormer windows. On the courtyard (inner) façade their pediments are cut out in a series of curves and counter-curves; on the outer façade the pilasters stand away from the window, not directly supporting the pediment but acting as buttresses in the same way as on the Gothic dormer windows at Meillant, Amboise, on the Louis XII wing at Blois, and elsewhere.

But by comparison with the Francis I wing at Blois, Azay gives evidence of more extensive infiltration by ultramontane ideas. Instead of the traditional vice it has a straight double staircase divided by a string wall – one of the earliest of its kind ever built on this side of the Alps. It is true that Chenonceaux and Nantouillet also have equally novel stair-cases, but the vaulting over them is of the older, ribbed type, whereas at Azay the influence of the new style extends even to the construction and decoration of the vaulting, which is embellished with large panels ornamented with medallions.

It is worth noting that in the course of time the straight staircase with a sculptured dome above it became one of the indispensable refinements of a noble mansion. The staircases at Villers-Cotterêts and at the Louvre are famous. But at Poncé-sur-le-Loir (Sarthe), it was a humble private citizen who felt the urge to add lustre to his home in the form of one of these lavish ornaments. The staircase he built in 1542, with its 136 carved panels – all different – is one of the finest amongst many of which the Renaissance castles can be justly proud.

2 | The Nantouillet Formula Ecouen

Although the new formula embodied in the porch at Gaillon was such an outstanding success it was by no means the only one produced by the masons of France in their efforts to adapt the type of ornamentation imported from Italy to contemporary French architectural styles.

Even in Gaillon itself a mixture of Italianate panelling and Gothic tracery can be found in the north-west and north-east galleries (fragments of which can still be seen in the courtyard of the Ecole des Beaux-Arts in Paris). A similar admixture occurs on the buttresses of the great spiral staircase at Chaumont, built by the Cardinal d'Amboise for his nephew Charles. All this was a natural development from the com-bined styles used on the pillars in the gallery of the Louis XII wing at Blois.

At Chenonceaux, built by Thomas Bohier between 1515 and 1522, the pilasters flanking the windows are flat and have Italianate capitals, but they are not superimposed; their vertical line is cut by the interposition of wide, bare wall-space between the windows at each floor. Chenonceaux, however, is an isolated case; it differs only in certain details from its contemporary and neighbour at Blois and was never copied; whereas the royal palace was copied by all and sundry. (See Plate xvııı.)

Nantouillet (Seine-et-Marne) was in the old province of Parisis, many miles from the Loire Valley. Its date (1512) is inscribed on the splayed jamb of a window on the ground floor and, therefore, like Chenonceaux, it is of the same period as the Francis I wing at Blois. It was built by Antoine Duprat, who became Chancellor of France on the accession of the young king in 1515. Its particular interest lies in the fact that the formula used in adapting Italian ideas to domestic French architecture was entirely different from that used at Gaillon.

The decoration of the façade is far more restrained than at Gaillon. The general rhythm is given, both on the outer faces and in the courtyard, by a series of tall, flat, bare pilasters without capitals, rising from the ground to the roof in a symmetrical mural pattern. These pilasters would seem to denote (as Sauvageot suggests) the transposition into the sphere of ornamentation of the buttresses used in Gothic architecture to carry the thrust of vaulted buildings, as shown, for example, in the rear wing at Ussé. The spaces between the floors are marked out by two lines of horizontal mouldings with a row of circles in between. The window-openings were made without any reference to the siting of the pilasters. And this fact is of considerable importance, for it was the first indication in France of a new conception of which there was no trace at Gaillon nor (later) at Blois; namely, that the general exterior design had become independent of the interior arrangement of the house.

The dormers, which were probably the principal decorative feature, have disappeared, and it is unfortunately impossible to comment on their style. The ornamental carving elsewhere is restrained and the Italian note is far from predominant. Panels of grotesques in the window-jambs are framed in Gothic mouldings, bottle-shaped at the base like the pillars of the galleries of the Louis XII wing at Blois; and on the balusters of the small staircase in the left-hand wing at Gaillon the wreathed colonnettes in the Flamboyant

xvı *Valençay*

style have composite capitals in the Italian style; superimposed pilasters make a timid appearance in the chevet of the chapel, which is built out from the rear face of the castle and is entirely Gothic. So far as the actual building is concerned, the straight staircase gives eager proof of a desire to follow the new style, but the Flamboyant Gothic dome above it is entirely traditional. Looking at the building as a whole, the rejuvenation of its style in no way appears to have been merely the work of the decorator; it takes on a specific architectonic character which was entirely absent from Gaillon.

It may appear surprising that it was the Gaillon and not the Nantouillet formula that was adopted for the Francis I wing at Blois, since Cardinal d'Amboise had been dead for some years and Chancellor Duprat was in power. The explanation would seem to be that William Pacherot and other ornamentists who were working at Gaillon when the porch was built there were either in the employ of the Crown or closely connected with it; and it was they who brought the Gaillon formula from Normandy to the banks of the Loire.

It is indeed a curious fact that the influence of the Loire school was slow in showing its effect at Nantouillet. The castle itself is surrounded by a chemise flanked by heavy brick towers and encircled by a moat, which was at one time spanned by a drawbridge. The entrance porch, built into the curtain wall, is certainly one of the latest additions to the building, and it clearly shows the influence of the 'Loire formula'. The postern and the huge pilasters flanking the gate are reminiscent of Chenonceaux, and the series of niches along the upper part of the porch have a clear affinity with those of the staircase of the Francis I wing at Blois.

So far as is known at present, Nantouillet had no imitators. It nevertheless plays an important part in the history of French civil architecture because, after a lapse of some ten years, it served as a model for Ecouen, which, unlike Nantouillet, had an immediate influence upon a number of other châteaux of its time.

Ecouen was the home of Anne de Montmorency and was begun at some time prior to his appointment as Constable of France on February 10th, 1538, that is to say, very soon after the death of Antoine Duprat (July 9th, 1535) if not during his lifetime. (See Plate XIV.) Its general plan is characteristic of the great châteaux of the French Renaissance and owes its inspiration – by way of Bury (now disappeared) – to the plan of Plessis-Bourré. It is a quadrilateral of which the front face has been built deliberately low in order to open up the courtyard behind it. (This front face was demolished in 1787 and replaced by a building of nondescript style.) The novel feature of the building is the replacement of the four traditional corner-towers by four square pavilions. Although one would hardly suspect it at first sight, this feature is in fact of Italian inspiration and is modelled (as Mr. Fritz Schreiber[1] has so clearly shown) on the villa of Poggio-Reale, built at the gates of Naples in 1487 by Guiliano da Majano. This villa took the form of a peristyle built round a courtyard and cantoned with square pavilions at the four corners. In actual fact Ecouen was not the first French château in which the towers were replaced by pavilions. The Château de Madrid (near Paris) was begun during 1528 some time before any work started at Ecouen, and it had square pavilions instead of round towers at its four corners. But Madrid, which was built on a very original plan not unlike that of Poggio-Reale, was a type of 'Italian' villa with openings on all sides through the galleries which enclosed it. This is in no way true of Ecouen, which is essentially a French castle still retaining at least some of its military features. It has turrets, for example, in the angled recesses formed between the projecting pavilions and the adjoining buildings; it is surrounded by a bastionated *fausse-braie* and by a moat (which has since been converted into gardens). And it is precisely because these traditional features of the French fortified castle have been so boldly emphasised that the replacement of the round tower by the pavilion is of such exceptional architectural interest.

The masons at Ecouen undoubtedly borrowed from their opposite numbers at Nantouillet (barely fifteen miles away) the general disposition of the façades of their château; that

---

[1] '*Die französische Renaissance-Architecktur und die Poggio-Reale-Variationen des Sebastiano Serlio*', Berlin, s.d., in-8° de 73 p.

is to say, the tall, bare pilasters without capitals rising from ground level to the gutters and forming a regular pattern over the walls; the double lines of mouldings between the floors, and the projections formed where pilasters and mouldings intersect. At Ecouen again – as at Nantouillet – the exterior decoration is quite independent of the position of the windows, which have been sited without reference to the pilasters.

Nevertheless, it is quite apparent that, in comparison with Nantouillet, Ecouen denotes a movement towards a simpler style. By about 1540 the ornate decoration imported from Italy had lost its vogue in France as it had already done some time before in Italy. Ecouen is quite free of grotesques, candelabra or Italianate capitals; there are no circles between the horizontal mouldings; the windows are taller, more elegant, and cut straight into the walls with no carving on the jambs. The general effect is austere and regal, all decoration having been relegated to the dormers and chimneys, which stand out in rich contrast to the bare severity of the walls and are some of the finest examples of French Renaissance in existence. It is indeed surprising that masons employed by a Constable of France should have been so unmindful of the examples of restraint being given at the time by the royal palaces such as Madrid (which was in course of construction) and the oval courtyard at Fontainebleau (which had been completed some ten years before) as to draw their inspiration from the Loire Valley. The fireplaces on the rear wing at Ecouen are modelled on those of Chambord. The lower part is decorated with a large tabernacle motif of equivalent mass to a dormer; two small columns support a projecting entablature surmounted by a small triangular pediment.

The dormers on the wings at the rear and on the left of the building follow the design of those in Touraine and Blésois; the Dutch-style gables on the outside of the left-hand wing are modelled on those used at Chenonceaux and Chambord to relieve the harshness of the dormers; and the pediments and tabernacles on the courtyard side are in their several ways variations of those surmounting the dormers of the inner façade of the Francis I wing at Blois. The rejuvenation of the style is above all apparent in the ornamental details; the

S-shaped supports of the candelabra being replaced by small round arches, and the acroteria embellished with vases.

This old château of Ecouen is indeed of absorbing interest from every point of view. Of its builder, Anne de Montmorency, the Papal Nuncio, in a letter dated August 22nd, 1547, had written that he was 'In word and deed the most French of Frenchmen ever known'. It can equally well be said of Ecouen that it was the most French of all Renaissance châteaux. It was the product of a transitional period. The heyday of the ornamentalists was over and French masons were taking it upon themselves to imitate an antique style of which they knew nothing. They were presumably at no pains to profit by the knowledge brought to France by Serlio, who had arrived at Court in 1541 to initiate the people of France into the principles of the Classical style.

Ecouen, however, was not yet completed when in about 1545 a new figure appeared on the scene; a man with a consummate knowledge of Roman art; who had no need to seek inspiration in the Loire Valley. The dormers he designed for the inner face of the left-hand wing bear no resemblance whatever to those of the other wings. The theme he created was completely new, although all its elements were drawn from the Classical age and were rigorously authentic in form. But he did more. He carefully selected his elements with a view to their suitability for the residence of a great soldier. The columns flanking the windows are Doric, which, according to Vitruvius, is essentially a masculine order. The Dutch-style gables and tabernacled motifs are gone; in their place is an heraldic field with crossettes at the corners, flanked by inverted volutes. The field itself is carved either with a winged lightning or with the arms of the Montmorency; above it a triangular pediment is formed by two shields resting on a bucranium; and to right and left of the group are two breast-plates resting on acroteria.

We have every reason to believe that the newcomer who designed these dormers was Jean Goujon, who, as is well known, was in the Constable's service in about 1545. There is also every reason to believe that his activities were in no way limited to re-designing the dormers. M. Pierre du Colombier (*Jean Goujon*, p. 47) makes the very plausible suggestion that a number of other minor additions were made to the building under his direction, including the small Doric porch in front of the door of the rear wing and the interior disposition of the chapel, which stands at the corner of the left wing. The porch is still standing; the altar and the wood panellings of the chapel are now at Chantilly.[1]

Anne de Montmorency, who had received his sword of office from Francis I on February 10th, 1538, became the most powerful figure in the country after the King himself. It was not surp rising, therefore, that his palace at Ecouen exercised considerable influence over the style of other châteaux of the period.

It would be an exaggeration, however, to suggest that it was copied as slavishly as was the Francis I wing at Blois. In 1540 the art of building was evolving too rapidly to give time to the new façades at Ecouen to set a new fashion. Its two characteristics most commonly imitated by others were, first, the almost complete suppression of any military features; and, second, the replacement of the corner towers by pavilions as well provided with window-openings as the rest of the building. The nobles of the court took the view, no doubt, that if the mighty commander of the King's armies no longer thought it necessary to give his palace the appearance of a fortress they were quite justified in following his example. Indeed, Henry II himself followed the same policy at the Louvre ten or fifteen years later in replacing the south-west tower by the 'King's Pavilion', which was completed in 1556.

From 1540 onwards corner-towers were considered to be outmoded. Those which still exist on a number of later châteaux in the Loire Valley, such as Villegongis, Valençay and Serrant, owe their survival to the influence of Chambord, which was very much behind the prevailing fashion. On the other hand, in several other châteaux built at the same period in Blésois or Touraine the contemporary style was closely followed, and towers were excluded.

Villandry and Villesavin were both built by Jean Le

---

[1] Later, during and after the reign of Henry II, some very considerable changes were made to the chapel by Jean Bullant; they will be referred to in a following chapter.

Breton, President of the Chamber of Audit of Blois. (The historian Bernier states that Le Breton had 'conducted the building of Chambord', which seems to be confirmed by the fact that after Jean Le Breton's death his widow, Anne Gedoyn, was granted by royal decree dated March 27th, 1543, the superintendence of the building of Chambord.) Le Breton's additional responsibilities, however, do not seem to have prevented him from following the new style; and his own two châteaux were apparently the first in the district to replace the traditional towers by pavilions.

Villandry has been so much restored that it is difficult to study it in detail. Villesavin, on the contrary, is well worth attention. Although small it has very great charm. It is a simple, one-storey building with a high roof, from which the dormers stand out in sharp relief. Its wings are arranged in a horseshoe pattern around a rectangular courtyard, the left-hand wing being simply a wall. Except for a ditch, the front of the courtyard seems always to have been completely unenclosed. The general plan is an exact copy of Ecouen: a square pavilion at each of the four corners, the left-hand front pavilion being the chapel. It is important to note that the date inscribed on the dormers of one of the front pavilions is 1537, that is to say, some time before Anne de Montmorency's new home at Ecouen was completed. One can say, therefore, that the plan of Villesavin represented a completely new conception in castle design. It is not claimed, of course, that it was the forerunner of Ecouen; but one may assume that Jean Le Breton had some knowledge of what was being done there. This impression is confirmed by the dormers on the right-hand wing, which have bowed pediments faced with a line of small leaves resembling *rais de cœur*.[1] The dormers on the outside of the rear wing at Ecouen have similar pediments, and they are clearly prior to February 10th, 1538, since there is as yet no sign of the Constable's sword on them; they differ only in detail from those of Villesavin by having a row of ovolos instead of *rais de cœur* along the edge of the pediment.

Although Villesavin, in our view, shows clear signs of

---

[1] A sculptured ornament composed of flowers and lance-heads.

outside influence, it is none the less an authentic 'Château of the Loire', for it has certain definitely local characteristics. The existence of an interior spiral staircase, for example, in the rear wing is rather unexpected in 1537 and can only be explained by the vicinity of Chambord, barely six miles away. There are also a number of similarities in the style of decoration. As at Blois, the windows are framed in super-imposed pilasters; and on the ground floor and in the dor-mers the capitals are in the Italian mode; the pinnacles are in the form of candelabra; there is a tendency towards excessive ornamentation; the pediments of the dormers are embellished externally with intricately carved volutes: and those on the right-hand wing are carved with large female figures, amongst which Mlle. Edith Guimblet (whose book on Villesavin is still in the manuscript stage) claims to identify the personages of tragedy, comedy and music.

La Morinière is about twelve miles south of Villesavin and is ten years younger than its neighbour. A fragment of iron-work from the chapel bearing the date 1548 has been trans-ferred to the entrance of the main building.

La Moriniére was built by René des Roches, whose wife was Ronsard's maternal aunt. He seems to have employed local masons, who copied generously from neighbouring châteaux. The red-brick walls, adorned with black-brick diamonds, are typical of the Louis XII wing at Blois; the dormers are copied from those of Chambord to the point even of imitating the slate discs on the white stone. From Cham-bord, too, came the idea of placing the spiral staircase inside the building, but no provision was made for lighting the shaft of the staircase and it became necessary later to cut an opening in it opposite one of the windows of the façade.

The general plan is obviously based on Villesavin. The house itself is an unpretentious building with neither towers nor pavilions, occupying the far side of a quadrangle sur-rounded by a filled moat. A square pavilion stands at each corner of the front of the quadrangle, the right-hand pavilion, which includes the chapel, being connected by a low wing to the house. The left-hand pavilion stands alone. It will be seen, therefore, that the only difference between La Mori-nière and Villesavin is that the left-hand wall enclosing the

courtyard at Villesavin has disappeared, so that the courtyard of La Morinière is open on two sides. It is interesting, in
the middle of the sixteenth century, to find an arrangement
of this kind, which was to recur nearly seventy-five years
later under Louis XIII, at Blérancourt and at Balleroy. Even
before 1550 the idea that a French château had any military
significance was being completely discarded; it was becoming
more and more a place of residence, open on all sides; and
the court of honour was becoming a thing of the past.

3 | The Bramante Style
Leonardo da Vinci: Chambord

At the time when the Gaillon porch and the Francis I wing at
Blois were being built the florid decoration used on their
façades was completely outmoded in Italy. Bramante (who
died in 1511) and Raphael (who died in 1520) had introduced completely new ideas into the art of building. They
revived the Classical style with its emphasis on a minute
study of the law of proportions, and had rejected every form
of excessive ornamentation as being in bad taste.

In December 1515, after the battle of Marignan, Francis I
had spent four days with Pope Leo X; and it is more than
likely that the embellishments being made to the Vatican
were discussed. It is in any case extremely interesting to find
at Blois on the outer façade (known as the *façade des Loges*) of
the Francis I wing an obvious imitation of Bramante's work
at the Vatican. The right-hand portion of the Blois façade
comprises two superimposed rows of Roman arches resting on
imposts, with pilasters between, and is certainly modelled on
the Saint Damaso courtyard. The left-hand portion is a copy
of the alternating arches and niches of the La Pigna courtyard. When the upper colonnade was added later the Saint
Damaso courtyard was again used as a model.

This is the first appearance in France of an attempt at the
Classical style, although it was executed in a very clumsy
manner. The King's masons evidently dared not risk building
two rows of arches one upon the other, so they erected
instead a thick wall into which deep bays were cut. In the

XVIII *Chenonceaux*

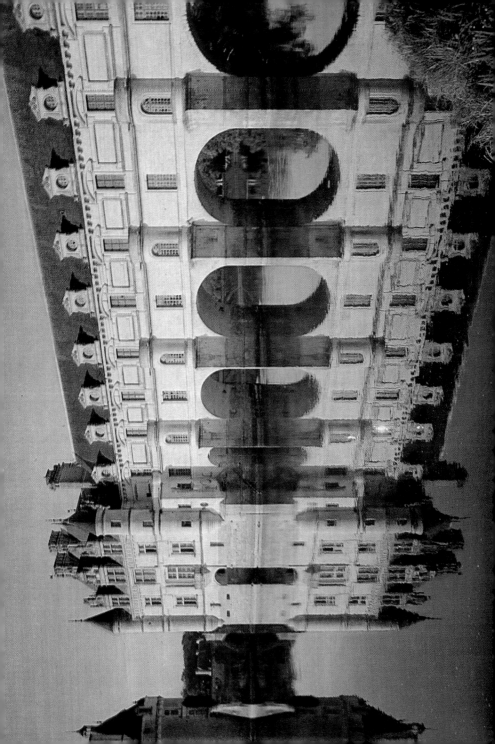

depth of the bays they made window-openings or 'loggias'; they then covered the wall with blind arches so small that they seem no more than mere ornamentation.

The French masons, however, soon became more skilful. A row of arches in the Roman style had been built on to the face of the low wall in front of the courtyard at Bury – which was contemporary with the Francis I wing. It has long since disappeared, but Du Cerceau evidently considered that the work was of sufficiently high standard to merit a large-scale engraving in his famous collection.

The progress shown between the *Façade des Loges* at Blois and the arcade at Bury is so remarkable that one is inclined to suspect that the masons at Bury must have been given not only scale drawings of the design but at the same time some technical advice from an outside source.

But who was able or likely to give such advice? The question raises a point which is still obscure and which it would be tempting to clarify if possible; for it concerns the part played in France by no less a person than Leonardo da Vinci.

Da Vinci is thought to have arrived in France in the autumn of 1516; he died at Amboise on May 2nd, 1519.

M. Heydenreich and other earlier writers think there is some justification in associating Leonardo da Vinci with the rebuilding of the castle of Romorantin. Three handwritten documents preserved in the Blois library (MSS. 269, 207 and 270) dated respectively 1770, 1818, and early nineteenth century, relate that Francis I undertook the enlargement of a small château at Romorantin belonging to his mother. The walls had reached a height of only 10 feet when the work was interrupted by an epidemic; it was never resumed. The same documents also state that a few vestiges of the walls were still standing before the French Revolution, but no description is given of them. The only guide to its date is a payment of £4,000 made by Francis I in 1518 on account of this work.

Certain passages, however, in Leonardo da Vinci's manuscripts (*Codex Atlanticus*, fol. 336 V° and *Codex Arundel*, pp. 269–70) show that Leonardo had a hand in certain projects concerning the canals and rivers in the Romorantin region;

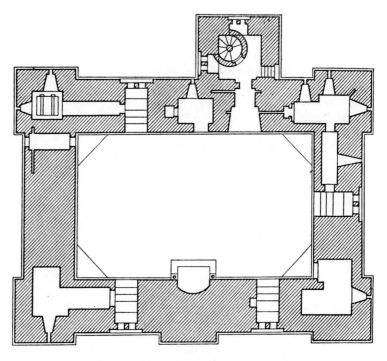

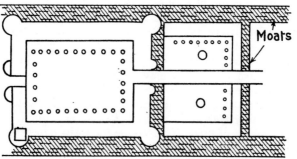

FIG. 4. (*above*) THE KEEP, CHAMBOIS (after *Rupuch-Robert*)
(*below*) LEONARD DA VINCI: "*Palazzo del principe*":
(*from the Ambrosian Library, Milan, codice atlantico, fol. 76, vº b.*)

and a note in the *Codex Atlanticus* (fol. 336 V°) states that he was at Romorantin at the same time as Francis I, a few days before the feast of Saint Antony. The exact date is not known, but it was probably in January, 1517.

The final evidence is on a page of the *Codex Atlanticus* (fol. 76 V°) which contains various notes about a building which Leonardo da Vinci calls *il palazzo del principe*. With these notes is a small plan of a rectangular château with towers at the corners, two gates each flanked by two towers and a central courtyard surrounded by a colonnade. The house lies along a canal or river and also a moat some 80 yards wide. Beyond the moat is a road described – but almost illegibly – *strada d'Ambosa* (road to Amboise). It is thought that this 'Prince's palace' is Leonardo da Vinci's project for the château of Romorantin, which was never built. (See p. 106.)[1]

All this, obviously, is obscure and conjectural and would hardly merit discussion without the further evidence of La Rochefoucauld.

This château was built by François, duc de la Rochefoucauld, who married in 1518 and died in 1533. The exact date is confirmed by the inscription 1528 on the entrance to the main staircase. The greater part of the house must have been built between 1520 and 1530, replacing a medieval fortress of which the old Norman-style keep and most of the fifteenth-century towers are still standing. The curtains of the south and east wings were remodelled to the style of the Châteaux of the Loire.

A remarkable feature – and unique in France – is the decoration of the courtyard by three superimposed galleries of arches in the manner of an Italian palace. It is obvious, too, that the architectural elements used were selected with great discernment. The double lines of mouldings between the floors, characteristic of the Loire Châteaux and of Nantouillet, have disappeared. Following the Bramante formula, each column has its complete entablature and is surmounted by a bare stylobate serving as a parapet for the

[1] A model of this castle was actually shown at the Leonardo da Vinci exhibition in Milan in 1939.

gallery above. All ornamentation is reduced to an austere minimum.

The inspiration behind this exceptional work is so obviously foreign that one is naturally inclined to be curious as to its source. It is quite possible that the masons were sent drawings from Italy. But one must remember that François, the first Duke of La Rochefoucauld and the father of the man who built the château, was godfather to King Francis I, and that he was also a friend and neighbour of Louise de Savoie when she lived at Cognac. It may, therefore, not be very far from the truth to imagine that da Vinci's *Palazzo del principe* (which never got beyond the planning stage at Romorantin) was eventually used as the plan of the château by the River Sauldre at La Rochefoucauld.

Marcel Reymond, in an article in the *Gazette des beaux-arts* of June, 1913, had suggested that Leonardo da Vinci may have had some part in building the most famous of all French Renaissance châteaux: Chambord. This suggestion was again brought forward at the Leonardo da Vinci Congress in 1952 by Dr. Lesueur and also by Mr. Ludwig Heydenreich, and should not now be considered as extravagant as it was when it was first propounded. It should be said at once, however, that any direct participation by Leonardo da Vinci in the actual building operations was out of the question. Work on Chambord probably began in September, 1519, four or five months after the artist's death on May 2nd, 1519. The laying of the foundations was complicated and prolonged; all work on the building had to be suspended for twenty-seven months during the Pavia campaign. It is our view that the keep (which was a leading feature of the château) was not built until some time between 1526 and 1533; the decoration of the upper storeys was not completed until about 1540, and certain of the wings were completed only during the reign of Henry II.

But although the actual building of Chambord took place after da Vinci's death, it had been preceded by a number of preliminary projects which must have been drawn up during the artist's lifetime; and it is most improbable that the King would not have sought da Vinci's advice upon them.

The general plan is obviously based on that of Vincennes.

It comprises an unusually long, low curtain wall measuring 170 yards by 128 yards, flanked by towers and surrounded by a *fausse-braie* and a moat. A massive keep, also flanked by corner towers, stands in the middle of one of the longer sides of the wall.

The keep, which is the most important part of the château, is a huge square building divided at each floor into two large rooms intersecting at right-angles to form four separate living apartments. The famous double spiral staircase winds up and through the building in such a way as to give direct access to each of these four apartments.

This strikingly original plan was, in fact, the result of a change made in a previous project that has since come to light, and which comprised a straight staircase in the Italian style occupying one of the arms of the cross formed by the intersection of the two large rooms as described above. It was later that the ingenious idea was conceived of replacing this straight staircase by a central spiral. Our own opinion is that this idea was Leonardo da Vinci's. There are several reasons for holding this view, but the main one is based on a comparison of two separate pieces of evidence. The first is a sketch with notes[1] by da Vinci himself, showing a staircase of his own invention consisting of four flights nesting one into the other. The second is a passage from Palladio, in the first book of his *Quattro libri dell'architettura*, to the effect that there was at Chambord a spiral staircase with four mutually-intersecting flights which gave direct access to four apartments in the middle of the building. Palladio's plan and the explanations given with it show that this quadruple staircase winding up through a great central shaft was lit from the interior in the same way as the staircases in the Pompey porticoes at Rome or the staircase built by Bramante in the Belvedere of the Vatican.

No quadruple staircase ever existed at Chambord; but the fact remains that Palladio was aware of the existence of a plan to build one. Da Vinci certainly knew of the spiral at the Belvedere and most probably of those in the Pompey porticoes. One must conclude, therefore, that he was the only

---

[1] In the library of the Institut de France, MS. B. fol. 47.

person who could have put forward the plan for a quadruple staircase at Chambord.

This plan (as we have already said) was never carried out. The French masons in charge of the work substituted for it a double staircase copied from that of the Saint Bernard monastery in Paris; and they enclosed it in a skeleton shaft. But the lantern on the roof of the keep may very well be a relic of the plan for an internally-lit spiral staircase. Although today it is a purely ornamental feature it would have been an indispensable part of the scheme if the staircase was to be lit from above.

As has already been said, Chambord was planned on the model of Vincennes. It is also typically French in the lavish treatment given to the upper parts of the building. In its general appearance it is reminiscent of the Duc de Berry's castles, and particularly of Méhun-sur-Yèvre, where the luxurious treatment of the upper floors contrasts sharply with the austerity of the building. The execution of the work is, understandably, in the Italian manner; but by the period 1530–40 the Italian manner was something very different from what it had been on the inner façade of the Francis I wing, or at Azay-le-Rideau. The ornamentation at Chambord is in keeping with the scale of the building, that is to say, it is related to large complete features such as a dormer, a chimney-stack, or the head of a staircase. The pilaster gives place to the more sturdy column. The panels of grotesques are gone and capitals are simpler in style except where they can be seen at close range. The whole scheme is enlivened by numbers of lozenges or discs of black slate inlaid in the white stone. The ornamental mason had clearly had his day; in Chambord, the last built of the Renaissance châteaux, we feel that the architect is coming into his kingdom.

Chambord was a very late example of the ornate Italian style and was out of fashion even before it was finished. Its influence at the time was slight, and in any case, purely local.

According to the date inscribed on some of its capitals, Villegongis was built in 1537, copying quite openly the style of decoration of the upper storeys of Chambord, with its slate discs inlaid in the white stone and even the design of its dormers and chimneys. The influence of Chambord can also be seen at Valençay, if only in the huge dimensions of this enormous building. The château comprises two wings set at right-angles; the west wing was not built until the seventeenth or eighteenth century; the north wing dates from the sixteenth century and is the only one which concerns us here. (See Plate XVI.)

Work on the building must have begun just after the marriage, on May 26th, 1540, of the lord of the manor, Jacques d'Etampes, to the daughter of a wealthy financier. The first part to be completed was the great tower at the north-west corner, which has the same gigantic proportions as the towers at Chambord. It also has the same type of decoration, with pilasters spaced at regular intervals against the walls and a double line of mouldings between the floors. The style changes in the adjoining wing under the influence of an evidently Classical urge; and the orders of the columns are made to follow Vitruvius's rule by the superposition of the Doric, Ionic and Corinthian. Next to it is the keep, which is a massive square building; its heavily and lavishly carved dormers and machicolations would suggest it was built at a later period – most probably during the reign of Charles IX. Beyond the keep the wing ends in a modest one-storey building and a small tower. The builders had evidently exhausted their resources before their wildly extravagant scheme could be completed.

4 | The Court in the Ile-de-France
Madrid: Fontainebleau: Saint Germain

Chambord, Villegongis and Valençay are in the old provinces of Blésois and Berry. It happened that just at the time they were being built the Court had left the Loire Valley. On his return from captivity Francis I, in letters dated March 15th, 1528, had announced his intention of 'setting up his home and spending his days for the most part in his good town and city of Paris and thereabouts'. By the end of April of that same year work had already begun on the royal palaces of the Bois de Boulogne (better known as Madrid) and at Fontainebleau.

Giròlamo della Robbia, who had arrived in France in

1518, played an important part in the building of the Château de Madrid (now completely disappeared). It was he who decorated the walls with glazed terracotta plaques similar to those used by his brother for the Ospedale del Ceppo at Pistoia. He also introduced on the façades a new architectonic style of Florentine origin, far more restrained than that of the Châteaux of the Loire. Superimposed pilasters and complicated pediments on dormers were suppressed; each window was given its own independent motif and was surmounted by a lintel and cornice or by a plain round pediment.

The influence of the new style at Madrid made itself very quickly felt, for terracotta medallions were being widely distributed from the Della Robbia workshop at Suresnes. A bust of the King appeared over the door of the small château at Sansac, near Loches (Indre-et-Loire). Further afield, medallions were used to decorate the façades of the château at Assier (Lot); and one should also mention, against the door in the west wing, a small window with a pediment in the Classical style, which in its elegant simplicity contrasts sharply with the Loire Valley style of the rest of the building. At Le Lude (Sarthe) the transition was less abrupt. M. Louis Hautecœur has pointed out that the new movement was given to the façades by adding large stone medallions imitating the terracotta plaques of the Della Robbia school.

Fontainebleau, unlike Madrid, was not a new building. All that was done there was to give an old castle a more modern air; in the process the original inner ward became the famous oval courtyard. The master-builder, Gilles Le Breton, was a man of limited ideas who succeeded only in creating a rather formless combination of components borrowed from elsewhere. From Chambord he adopted the regular lines of pilasters for the walls; from Madrid the triangular pediments on the dormers. The banality of the general theme was somewhat enlivened at a later stage by the addition of a peristyle over a passage along the façades and by the famous 'Serlio Portico' which was neither a portico in the strict sense of the word, nor was it by Serlio. M. A. Bray has established the fact that its upper storey was originally the landing of an outside staircase that was suppressed some ten years later.

XIX *Joinville, Le Grand Jardin*

The truth is that the building itself was only a secondary consideration. What Francis I really required from his builders was an appropriate setting for a scheme of decoration which should rival those of the Vatican and the Palazzo del Té at Mantua. With this in mind he sent for the two Italian artists, Rosso and Primaticcio, who arrived in France in 1530 and 1532 respectively.

The discovery of a combination of paintings with very low relief stucco in the 'Esquiline caves' at Rome had led these two men to imagine an entirely new type of decoration designed to give new emphasis to sculptured ornamentation used in conjunction with frescoes. The greater part of their work can still be seen – although the paintings have been restored – in the Francis I Gallery at Fontainebleau, where Rosso worked from 1543 until his death on November 14th, 1540. One is immediately struck by the similarity between the general composition of this gallery and that of the Sixtine Chapel at the Vatican, where the same effect is produced by framing the scenes from Genesis on the ceiling in a number of large figures and painted representations of statues.

When Fontainebleau was enlarged later by the addition of the White Horse courtyard (after Rosso's death) Primaticcio gave up the formula they had used for the Francis I Gallery. From 1541 until his death in 1570 he was engaged in covering the walls and ceiling of the huge Ulysses Gallery (since disappeared) with small-scale decoration in the manner of the Raphael Loggias at the Vatican, imitating the ancient grotesques unearthed in Rome.

The Fontainebleau School as represented by the Francis I and the Ulysses Galleries was copied subsequently in a number of private buildings. The Francis I Gallery was undoubtedly the model for the Aeneid Gallery in the left wing at Oiron (Deux-Sèvres) and also for the ornamentation of about ten fireplaces at Ecouen, where the principal subjects in the paintings are framed in cartouches. This decoration, however, was not carried out until the reign of Henry II. By this time Primaticcio was evolving a simpler style than Rosso's and forbidding the use of high-relief stucco. At Ecouen and Oiron, therefore, the stucco sculptures have disappeared and the large figures framing the picture are painted like frescoes

xx *Anet, The Dome of the Chapel*   H

in the same way as the principal subjects in the picture itself.

Although less pretentious than the decoration of the Francis I gallery, the grotesques in the Ulysses Gallery became very popular on account of the graceful effect they produced and also because they could be used so easily. The demand for them was countrywide, and one finds traces of them today in the most unlikely places, such as the oratory at Le Lude (Sarthe), the study at Pibrac (Haute-Garonne), as well as in the great rooms at Ancy-le-Franc (Yonne).

Except for the rear wing, the buildings in the White Horse courtyard at Fontainebleau were all designed by Pierre Chambiges, who, some time after 1540, also built the château at Saint Germain-en-Laye (Seine-et-Oise). The common characteristic of both buildings is the polychromatic treatment of the façades by a novel combination of brick and stone, the background being in stone and brick being used for pilasters, wall-arcades, and windows, etc. The idea obviously came from Italy, where coloured marble was being used in a similar way. The round-arch windows with their triangular pediments at Saint Germain, for example, bear a striking resemblance to those of the Scuola di San Marco at Venice.

This novel use of colour combinations became quite popular, and was immediately adopted for another royal mansion, la Muette (Seine), also by Pierre Chambiges, built between 1542 and 1549 and demolished in the seventeenth century. Later on, under Henry II, it again appears in the very fine courtyard at Fleury-en-Bière, which Dom Guillaume Morin, writing in 1630, attributes to Pierre Lescot. It will be found again, later still, under Henry IV at the Cour des Offices at Fontainebleau.

5 | First attempts in imitation of the Classical Style: Villers-Cotterêts

With one exception, all the Renaissance châteaux we have studied so far draw their inspiration from contemporary Italian architecture; and this is equally true of the ornate style of the Loire school, the more sober style of Madrid, and of imitations of the Bramante style.

The exception is the so-called Serlio Portico built in 1531 in the oval courtyard at Fontainebleau. The upper part of it is a copy – albeit a somewhat crude one – of a typical triumphal Roman arch with three rows of arches. Serlio's less ambitious building clearly owed nothing to contemporary styles; it shows a definite desire to return to the Classical school.

The same influence becomes quickly apparent in studying the royal château at Villers-Cotterêts, begun by Francis I in 1532. The main façade breaks with the traditional super-imposed pilasters and follows the theme of two orders in bold relief, with square pillars on the ground floor and columns backed against the floor above. A very significant change is noticeable in the capitals both of the pillars and columns. Instead of the Italianate Composite an obvious effort has been made to reproduce the Ionic capital on the pillars of the ground floor, while the capitals of the columns above are almost authentically Corinthian.

The 'Serlio Portico' and Villers-Cotterêts marked the beginning of a very important movement in French Renais-sance architecture towards a revival of the styles of the Classical age. This movement was encouraged by the publica-tion, in 1530, 1539, and 1542 of three editions of Diego de Sagredo's translation into French of the shortened version of Vitruvius' work. Its results were seen in widely scattered examples all over the country.

The château of Fontaine-Henri, near Caen (Calvados), was being rebuilt in the Flamboyant style when, in 1537, a well-known Caen architect, Blaise Le Prestre, took over the work. Against the windows on the west front of the main pavilion he replaced the traditional superimposed pilasters by columns standing on stylobates and having projecting entablatures; it is interesting to note, however, that the capitals are Italianate. (See Plate xv.)

At Assier (Lot), many miles from Normandy, the entrance to the château was decorated in 1535 both internally and externally with two porticoes in which the Ionic Order was superimposed on the Corinthian in accordance with Cesare Cesariano's *Vitruvius*, published in 1521.

It was not long before the rule regarding the super-position of the Orders was being followed in other buildings, and columns were used on the façades in a manner similar to that of Villers-Cotterêts. At the same time each new building showed an improvement on the royal one in the sense that the Classical style was being more accurately followed. At Mesnières (in Normandy) for instance – built in 1545 – the columns are fluted, the Ionic order being used on the ground floor and the Corinthian on the floor above. Again, the north wing at Bournazel (Aveyron), dated 1545, is attractively decorated with carved ornamentation but the correct disposition of the Orders is scrupulously followed. On the ground floor the columns are Doric, with the frieze of the entablature divided by triglyphs and metopes; on the floor above the columns are Ionic and the frieze finely decorated with Roman style foliations. Yet another example may be seen in Touraine at Le Grand-Pressigny; the gallery there, dated about 1550, is severely Classical almost to a point of excess, producing a somewhat chilling effect.

6 | Serlio

The arrival of the Bologna architect, Serlio, at the French Court in 1541 was an event of far greater importance than the publication of the French version of Vitruvius' works. From patient and careful study of antique ruins Serlio had redis-covered the science of correct proportions and had formulated a set of basic rules governing Classical architecture. It was this new learning which he now brought to France.

His influence made itself felt at once in the Grotte des Pins at Fontainebleau (1543) and in the balustrade surmounted by great vases on the terrace at Saint-Germain-en-Laye. His colleagues at Court, however, were by no means eager to welcome the intrusion of this foreigner whom they were expected to consider as a master, and in due course they made a point of denying him any part in their activities.

The result was a repetition – at the end of Francis I's reign – of what had happened under Louis XII. The development of architecture in France was no longer being directed by the

XXI *Chantilly, Le Châtele*

Crown; the initiative in new and advanced ideas had passed
into the hands of the private builder.

Serlio put his ideas into practical form in 1546 by building
for the brother-in-law of Diane de Poitiers the famous
château of Ancy-le-Franc. Pierre du Colombier and Pierre
d'Espezel (*Gazette des beaux-arts*, July 1934) have shown that
Serlio was the first – and probably the only – architect
employed on the building.

Ancy-le-Franc is a quadrilateral with square pavilions at
each corner, surrounded by a wide moat spanned at one time
by two drawbridges. It represents exactly the type of French
château an Italian architect would design in the middle of
the sixteenth century. Its very restrained exterior theme of
Doric pilasters with alternate window-openings and closed
bays recalls (as has often been observed) that of the Palace of
the Chancellery at Rome. The more ornately decorated
façades on the courtyard are an echo of the Pignia Court at
the Vatican; between the openings are Corinthian pilasters
with fluted shafts framing shell-shaped niches, which have
since been replaced (on the ground floor) by marble panels.
(See Plate XVII.)

Another example of a private building embodying advanced ideas in design was the château of Saint-Maur (Seine),
built for Cardinal Jean du Bellay probably a short time before
Ancy-le-Franc. It is particularly interesting to note that the
architect, Philibert Delorme, was French and had recently
returned from Rome where he had gone to study *in situ* the
secrets of antiquity. Saint-Maur (which has since disappeared)
was the product of a young mind and was a model of architectural skill. It was very strongly marked by Italian influence
– even more perhaps than Ancy-le-Franc. No dormers; no
high French roofs. Instead, a very flat roof masked by an
attic-order which, for good measure, was even painted with
frescoes.

The success of these imaginative and clever new designs
was immediate. The very attractive Grand-Jardin, which
Claude de Guise ordered to be built in 1546 at Joinville
(Haute-Marne), has points of resemblance with Ancy-le-
Franc, but even more notably (in its proportions and its
principle of a raised ground floor) with Saint-Maur. But

Grand-Jardin differs from both in the wealth and delicacy of its carving on the stylobates of the pilasters, on the friezes, the window-rails, and on the panels of the cornices. Like its contemporary at Bournazel, Grand-Jardin retains all the vitality of spirit of the early Renaissance. The men who built these châteaux, the one in Champagne and the other in Rouergue, enlivened the Vitruvian theme with a rich and ornate decoration, and produced two of the most charming creations of the French Renaissance period. (See Plate XIX.)

7 | The Reign of Henry II The Great Masters

Philibert Delorme's achievement at Saint-Maur showed that there were men in France whose knowledge of what was called 'real' architecture was as complete as that of the Italian masters.

On August 2nd, 1546, Francis I, who was nearing the end of his reign, had the great satisfaction of being able to entrust the rebuilding of the Louvre to one of his own subjects, Pierre Lescot, an architect of the new school. A few months later, on March 31st, 1547, Francis I died. His successor, Henry II, was evidently aware, however, that it was a matter of national importance to infuse some new blood into his staff, and on April 3rd, 1548, he appointed Philibert Delorme as superintendent of all Crown building operations. Encouraged by the King's support, the new school seized the opportunity afforded by his official entry into Paris on June 16th, 1549, of making a striking demonstration of their existence. Under Jean Goujon's direction a number of temporary buildings were erected to mark the Royal occasion; their impact on the world of art was as significant as the publication of Du Bellay's famous *Deffence et illustration de la langue françoise* had been on the world of letters two months earlier.

From this point onwards the Classicists dominated French Renaissance architecture, and its development can be summarised in the work of four great masters: Pierre Lescot and Jean Goujon (working together), Philibert Delorme and

Jean Bullant. Pierre Lescot's only Royal commission was for
the Louvre; in 1546 he was entrusted with the rebuilding of
the west wing of the old medieval castle. (This wing now
stands on the south side of the Pavillon de l'Horloge in the
courtyard of the Louvre.) Between 1551 and 1556 he built
the Pavilion du Roi, replacing the old south-west tower of
Phillip-Augustus' fortress. Once this work was completed
the King ordered him to rebuild the south wing of the old
castle in the same new style.

The simplicity of Pierre Lescot's main theme for the façade
of the new west wing is a model of Classical architecture. It
consists of two orders of Corinthian pilasters supported on
stylobates, and surmounted by entablatures with an attic
order above. The monotony of the horizontal lines is relieved
by frontispieces at the centre and at each end of the façade.
These projecting features stand out very discreetly, the whole
effect being obtained by using coupled columns instead of
pilasters. Jean Goujon then proceeded to embellish this theme
with sculptured ornamentation in the Classical style, very
rich, but in faultless taste. This decoration is, in fact, essential
to the architectural scheme, which would otherwise appear
too bare; and one wonders if Jean Goujon, who was reputed
to be *studieux d'architecture*, had not some share in the composition of the whole work.

There can be no question, however, of any participation by
Jean Goujon in the King's Pavilion. The sober decoration of
its façade was obviously inspired by the Palazzo Farnese in
Rome, for it has the same plain horizontal mouldings between
the floors, the same heavily rusticated stonework at the
quoins, and is similarly bare of all orders.

The Pavillon du Roi was masked by a new front in the
seventeenth century and is therefore no longer visible; but its
counterpart can still be seen many miles to the south in the
Vaucluse department, at La Tour-d'Aigues. This great castle
was rebuilt in 1560 on the plan of an immense quadrilateral
with square pavilions right and left of the entrance and round
towers at the rear corners. The old keep of the original castle,
which stands in the middle of the courtyard, was preserved
and given a measure of exterior decoration to conform to the
style of the newer buildings. The castle today is in a ruinous

state, but the pavilion on the left-hand side of the entrance is still standing. The similarity with its prototype at the Louvre is apparent not only in the composition as a whole but also in the absence of orders, the mouldings between the floors, the lines of rusticated stonework at the quoins, its attic storey, and even the design of the mouldings. It differs only in the crowning, which is an imitation of one of the frontispieces added by Jean Bullant to the castle of Ecouen. The design he executed in 1571 for this famous porch at the entrance to La Tour-d'Aigues was clearly of Classic origin, suggested no doubt by the Roman monuments which still exist in that region. The idea for the great corner pilasters came from the bridge at Saint-Chamas (Bouches-du-Rhône), and the trophies on the frieze have much in common with the decoration of the triumphal arch at Orange (Vaucluse).

Another château which may well have been the work of Pierre Lescot was at Vallery (Yonne), the home of the extravagant and dashing Marshal de Saint-André. Work began in about 1550 and continued until the Marshal's death on December 19th, 1562. M. Pierre Colombier records a contract dated May 5th, 1556, by which Pierre Lescot was put in charge of operations on one of the pavilions in the gardens. It is not clearly established that he was also responsible for the building of the house itself, but this would appear likely from the conspicuous skill and attention given to every detail of the work. Du Cerceau claims that the corner pavilion at Vallery has a common quality with that of the Louvre, 'not in its design as a whole, but in the beauty and excellence of every part'.

The château was never finished. Of the two wings originally built all that remains today is one wing with its corner pavilion. The style is extremely sober; brick and stone are used in the traditional manner of Plessis-lès-Tours and Blois, with no attempt at any new combinations. The stone stands out in sharp relief against a background of brick. There is no sculptured ornamentation; on the contrary, the emphasis is on vigour and strength, symbolised by the heavy rustication of the stone facings. The lines are clean and robust, an anticipation – in the sixteenth century – of the style destined to become so popular under Henry IV and Louis XIII.

Philibert Delorme eventually rose to a position of considerable influence at Court, but much of his work seems to have become the victim of a malignant fate.

Some time after 1547, during the reign of Henry II, he built the Château of Anet (Eure-et-Loir) for Diane de Poitiers. Very little of it has survived, but from what remains it is possible to learn something of the style of this famous building.

It comprised three courtyards in line from east to west, the middle one being the court of honour. The front wing followed tradition in being lower than the others. In order to preserve the unity of the building Delorme had the happy idea of joining the three courts by a common façade. The front wing, dated 1552, is still standing. The architect showed great skill in avoiding a generally monotonous effect by using a succession of features of varying depth and a series of levels at unequal heights. The walls to right and left are of brick and stone; in the centre is the magnificent entrance of stone and inlaid black marble surmounted by a balustrade of interlacing tracery framing Benvenuto Cellini's famous nymph (now replaced by a plaster casting, the original being in the Louvre).

Delorme gave ample proof of his inventive genius not only in this wing but throughout the building; and he used every possible source as a stimulant for his imaginative faculties. From Classical antiquity he adopted the porch, with its three superimposed Orders built against the façade of the rear wing (now preserved in the courtyard of the Ecole des Beaux-Arts in Paris); from Italy he took his design for the chapel, which is all that remains of the right-hand wing and could have been the work of one of the Italian masters; and, above all, he drew upon national pride by retaining military features in his design. The buildings are surrounded by a ditch; the corner pavilions are on a bastioned plan; there are watch-towers on the corners of the surviving left-hand wing; there are numerous gun-embrasures on all the approaches to the house, and at the so-called *Charles-le-Mauvais* gate the gargoyles on these embrasures have the form of a cannon.

Delorme drew his ideas, then, from these many and varied sources; but he was able to create from them an integrated,

essentially personal style. So far as his general composition
was concerned his chief object was movement. This is clearly
evident in every feature of the front wing; it is equally noticeable on what remains of the left-hand wing, in the rhythm
created by the alternating large and small dormers. In
contrast to Pierre Lescot's treatment of the Louvre, Delorme
eschewed ornamentation and gave only negligible opportunity to the sculptor. In his view, decoration in all its forms
was the exclusive concern of the architect, and he had the gift
of using every possible circumstance to serve his purpose.
From the initials and emblems associated with Diane de
Poitiers he created an enormous variety of motifs such as
deltas, crescents, bows, arrows and quivers; and over the
fireplaces and dormers and on the pedestal of the fountain of
Diana he portrayed the tomb which the King's favourite had
adopted as her emblem after his death.

It is not surprising that Philibert Delorme also claimed, as
architect, responsibility for the interior decoration of the
rooms. As a result of his search for new ideas in competition
with his rivals Rosso and Primaticcio at Fontainebleau he
greatly developed the use of woodwork and designed some
richly coffered ceilings. On occasion he actually covered the
whole room – walls, ceiling and floor – with wood panelling
and parquet. Practically nothing has survived of all this
splendour at Anet; but at Fontainebleau the magnificent
coffered ceiling installed by Delorme in the ballroom in
1550 has been preserved. Another example of a completely
panelled room can also be seen today in the 'Cabinet des
Grelots' (dated 1553) at the small château of Beauregard,
near Blois. The restrained, polished style of its architecture
suggests that it was the work of a master – who may have been
Philibert Delorme himself.

Jean Bullant, like Philibert Delorme, had studied art in
Rome; the two men represent similar schools of thought.
Jean Bullant had spent the greater part of his life in the
service of the Constable, Anne de Montmorency, and had
worked for him at Ecouen and Chantilly. By a happy stroke
of fortune nearly all his works have been preserved.

He carried out a number of modifications at Ecouen,
which had just been built. The first of these – which took

place during the reign of Henry II – was to re-design in the Classic style the outer façade of the right-hand (north) wing. This was followed by a series of frontispieces laid on to the middle of the façades; first, on the inner façade of the right-hand wing, a frontispiece of columns bearing the arms of Henry II; next – on the outer façade of the same wing – another similar feature, but without the royal arms. Two other features (which do not appear on Du Cerceau's plan) were evidently added later: the great gateway (since disappeared) of the east wing, and the famous porch of four Corinthian columns on the left-hand wing (a gesture of architectural bravura which inaugurated a vogue for the Corinthian order in France).

The 'châtelet' at Chantilly was built alongside the main château in 1560. The unity and harmony of Jean Bullant's composition was achieved by his evident concern to avoid monotony and to enliven the whole theme without departing from the Classical rule. The semi-dormer windows give movement to each façade, and each façade is different from the rest. The western side is decorated with gigantic pilasters, which are no doubt of earlier date than the porch at Ecouen; the south side, overlooking the lake, is embellished with a balcony running along the water's edge (Louis Hautecœur describes it as a kind of *fausse-braie*); and in the courtyard the semi-dormers on the first floor alternate with the windows of the ground floor, giving an unexpected chessboard effect. By this ingenious arrangement of the various architectural features and without the use of carved ornamentation of any kind the architect succeeded in making this small building one of the most charming châteaux of the French Renaissance. (See Plate XXI.)

8 | The End of the Sixteenth Century

During the second half of the sixteenth century a number of plans were prepared for what M. Louis Hautecœur calls *les grandes compositions*, that is to say, of châteaux comprising a number of buildings integrated into one vast edifice. Most of these grandiose compositions either failed to go beyond the planning stage or were only partially completed. In many cases even those parts that had been completed – Les Tuileries, for example, and Verneuil – have disappeared. At Chenonceaux, however, the work done at that time – little as it was – has survived and can still be seen.

Chenonceaux had been built in about 1520 on the piers of an old mill by Thomas Bohier,[1] 'Général des Finances'. Thirty-five years later it was acquired by Diane de Poitiers and a bridge was built connecting it with the left bank of the Cher river. After the death of Henry II it came into the possession of Catherine de Médicis who, in 1576, ordered plans to be drawn up – probably by Jean Bullant – for large-scale extensions and alterations to the house. Of the numerous buildings included in these plans only the wing on the forecourt (known as *les dômes*) and the three storeys of galleries on the bridge were actually begun; and they were not completed until after Jean Bullant's death. The famous galleries probably date from 1579 or 1580. Their more notable features include the semicircular watch-towers erected on the projecting spurs of the piers of the bridge. In 1579 Baptiste du Cerceau and Pierre Desilles produced plans for similar structures on the Pont Neuf in Paris. It is quite possible that the architects concerned at each place were not entirely ignorant of the others' plans. In any case it was common practice in the Middle Ages to build watch-towers on the piers of fortified bridges; as is seen on the approach bridge at the castle of Méhun-sur-Yèvre. (See Plate XVIII.)

It is quite understandable that the original grand design for Chenonceaux never materialised. When the galleries on the bridge were built France was in the throes of the religious wars; it seemed an ill-chosen moment for building unprotected houses. It was felt, on the contrary, that provision should be made for defence against a surprise attack; and therefore the military works that appeared on certain castles at that time were no longer merely symbolic or ornamental, they were authentic and serviceable organs of defence.

One of the most striking examples of late fortification of

---

[1] Financial Controller of Normandy under Francis I.

XXIII *Balleroy*

this kind is at Kerjean in Brittany. This great granite castle was built on a plan similar to that of Ecouen. It is a quadrilateral closed in front by a plain low wall with a terrace built against it. There are four corner pavilions, one of which – on the front façade – contains the chapel. The rear wing is in very sober style, the architectural effect being sustained entirely by the elegant proportions of the windows. Judging by the crescents surmounting the dormers of the pavilion where the staircase is housed, this rear wing was built during Henry II's reign. The style of the lateral wings is much less severe, suggesting that they were of a slightly later date. Although the entrance itself is in the form of a triumphal arch it is the front façade of the castle that is organised for defence. Both the heavy wall shutting off the courtyard and the bases of the adjoining pavilions are riddled with gun-embrasures. What is more, the castle is surrounded at some distance from it by a fortified *enceinte* formed by a wide rampart strengthened with numerous casemates and flanked by a flat-bottomed ditch. This *enceinte* has corner towers surmounted by strangely old-fashioned machicolations and pierced with two doors defended at one time by drawbridges. It is possible that this rampart stands on the site of a former curtain wall, but it was certainly rebuilt in the sixteenth century, for on the south door the arms of the owner, Louis le Barbier, are still visible; he died in 1596.

xxiv *Cheverny, The Front Façade*

CHAPTER THREE

THE POST-RENAISSANCE |

1 | New work on the Louvre and Fontainebleau

Unlike Henry III, Henry IV had a passion for building, and took pleasure in showing his friends round his castles; he also had a predilection for grandiose compositions.

Immediately after his entry into Paris in March 1594, he gave orders for work to be resumed on the Louvre. The main object was to connect the castle of the Louvre (which had been partially rebuilt by Pierre Lescot) with the palace of the Tuileries built by Catherine de Médicis over a period of years between 1564 and 1572. A start had been made, about 1566, with the work of joining up the two buildings, but the Small Gallery built at that time from the Louvre to the Seine was no more than a ground-floor passage with a terraced roof.

The new work was put in hand in January, 1595, but it made slow progress and was not completed until 1610. It comprised two main projects: the addition of an extra floor to the Small Gallery, and the building of the immense Grand Gallery along the river, terminating in the Pavillon de Flore at the junction with the Tuileries. The Galerie des Rois (that is to say, the new first floor of the Small Gallery) was destroyed by fire in 1661 and replaced by the Galerie d'Apollon, designed by Le Brun.

126

The Grand Gallery along the river had not at that time
the uniformity of style that it has today. It was intersected by
the city walls built by Charles V, which followed the bank of
the Seine from the Louvre up to the present entrance to the
Place du Carrousel and then turned at right-angles north-
wards. The eastern section of the new building (inside the
city walls) followed the line of the *enceinte* and has survived
more or less unchanged to this day. Its façade is heavily
ornamented with vermiculated rustication, high-relief friezes,
pilasters, niches, and alternating triangular and semicircular
pediments. The gallery itself occupies the upper floor. Henry
IV used the lower floors (the ground floor and the entresol)
to house his team of craftsmen within the secluded precincts
of the Court well away from the tyrannical influence of the
craft guilds. The western section of the Gallery (outside the
city walls) was probably the work of the second Jacques du
Cerceau. His design for its façade consisted of immense
coupled pilasters surmounted by alternate triangular and
semicircular pediments. This façade was destroyed under the
Second Empire, but a copy of it can be seen on the façade of
the north gallery in the Place du Carrousel.

These two galleries were the only additions made to the
Louvre by Henry IV, although his plans for the building had
been far more ambitious. His intention was to quadruple the
size of the courtyard and to build another great gallery connecting the Louvre with the Tuileries. (This gallery was not
built, in fact, until the nineteenth century.)

Henry IV's dream of quadrupling the size of the Louvre
did not materialise during his own lifetime; but the project
was taken in hand by Louis XIII. The work went on from
1624 to 1627 and was directed by Jacques le Mercier, who
extended the west wing and repeated on its north side the
façade designed by Pierre Lescot in 1546. Between the old and
the new buildings he erected the Pavillon de l'Horloge to
form the central motif of the whole wing. With considerable
skill and good taste Le Mercier succeeded in giving this
pavilion its necessary mass in relation to the rest of the building without detracting from the value of Pierre Lescot's
façade. The three lower floors of the pavilion are well
matched with Lescot's sixteenth-century design; but on the

floor above – which was added to give additional relief to the pavilion – a slight suggestion of the architect's leanings toward the Baroque is visible in the tall, twin cariatides (inspired no doubt by Verneuil) in the three interlocking pediments and in the four-cornered dome crowning the building. It must be admitted, however, that in spite of Le Mercier's skill and artistry the quadrupling of the old Louvre was a mistake; Pierre Lescot's façade had been designed for a courtyard one quarter of its present size and is, therefore, out of proportion with the building as a whole.

In addition to the Louvre Henry IV carried out a number of building operations in other royal palaces. At Fontaine-bleau, in particular, the oval court was re-planned, the eastern end being closed by a plain low wall. Following the prevailing mode, a monumental pavilion – the Baptistry – was added at the centre. In front of this entrance a new court was built ('La Cour des Offices') in a very simple style and decorated with brick courses in a similar manner to that of the White Horse Courtyard.

When the work on the oval court was finished the royal apartments were installed there. The decoration in one of the rooms – the 'Louis XIII' room – has been preserved and has something in common, in its general theme, if not in the manner of execution, with the Francis I Gallery. The walls are divided horizontally into two parts. The lower part is covered with high panelling, not in natural wood as in the Francis I Gallery, but in a large number of small painted panels of attractive landscapes and flowers. The upper part is decorated with a series of pictures separated one from the other by heavily ornamented stucco moulding and depicting various incidents in the story of Theogenes and Chariclea.

2 | Private Mansions

Henry IV was not only a great builder himself; he encouraged the nobility to build and, above all, to build great houses. He was indeed at times embarrassingly insistent on this point. According to Girard (historian to the duc d'Epernon) he went so far as to commission one of his architects to draw up the plans of Cadillac. Pierre du Colombier points out that the encouragement thus given to the rural nobility was the result of a definite 'back-to-the-land' policy jointly instigated by the King and Sully. In spite of the ruin and desolation caused by the religious wars, a new moneyed class was emerging; and the combination of these factors with the encouragement given in official quarters led to the building of a considerable number of châteaux during the first half of the seventeenth century. There seems little evidence that private building followed the style of the royal palaces, which, in any case, would have been unsuitable for the purpose. For the most part the work undertaken was in the nature of additions or improvements to existing properties. It is true that the huge double pilasters on the façade of Effiat (Puy-de-Dôme), built in 1627, might have been copied from the extra-mural portion of the Grand Gallery of the Louvre; but this imitation of a Crown building must be considered as a rare exception to the general rule. The influence of the Royal palaces, so far as building styles were concerned, was far less than that of the great schemes of urban reconstruction which were carried out in Paris by Henry IV and did so much to beautify the city. The Place Royale (now the Place des Vosges) was begun in 1605; in 1607 the President of the French Parliament, Achille de Harlay, was made responsible for the construction of the Place Dauphine.

The colourful charm of these buildings, with their happy blending of brick, stone and slated roofs, has made them universally famous. We know, too, the enthusiasm they aroused at the time in Paris and elsewhere.

Sully, in his capacity as controller of roads and highways, had been the final authority in the production of these two schemes. It is also significant that in about 1600 he had begun to rebuild his ancestral home at Rosny (Seine-et-Oise) and that its brick-and-stone façades and slate roofs bore a striking resemblance to those used later on the Place Royale. There are very cogent reasons, therefore, for thinking that Sully was largely responsible for creating and popularising this new style. No documentary evidence exists to identify the architect or architects who drew up the plans either for Rosny or for the two public squares in Paris. M. Baudson has suggested

I

that it was Louis Métezeau, but he offers no proof in support of this claim.

What is even more puzzling, however, is the fact that certain writers find it so difficult to discover the sources of this particular style. Some have even gone so far as to suggest that its austerity was a reflection of the Huguenot mentality!

The fact is that there can be no question as to its origin, for the brick-and-stone theme was in no way a novelty in France in the early years of the seventeenth century. Even in the middle of the fifteenth century (as we have seen) it was already being used by Charles d'Orléans at Blois, and also at Plessis-lès-Tours. We find it again a century later, with all the vigour and austerity so characteristic of the Louis XIII style, in Marshal de Saint André's home at Vallery; and again in 1586, equally austere, in Cardinal de Bourbon's abbatial palace of Saint-Germain-des-Prés in Paris. Far from being a striking innovation, what we now call the Louis XIII style was merely the evolution of a long-established tradition.

It would seem appropriate here to add (as a general comment) that the wars of religion, although they called a temporary halt to the development of French architecture, did not constitute a break with the past. The French châteaux of the beginning of the seventeenth century were clearly the descendants of those of the Classical Renaissance. If this is borne in mind it will be less difficult to unravel later the apparent confusion in their styles.

3 | Châteaux of Traditional Design

The great châteaux of Cadillac, Brissac and Vizille were built to the order of three noblemen of very high rank. Cadillac was built by the duc d'Epernon, Henry III's favourite; Brissac by Marshal Charles de Cossé-Brissac, who had opened the gates of Paris to Henry IV in 1594; and Vizille by the duc de Lesdiguières, later to be promoted to the rank of Constable of France. All three châteaux were built in stone and they have kept to this day a somewhat military air. Cadillac, of which the first stone was laid on August 4th, 1599, still followed the Renaissance style exemplified by

xxv *Grosbois*

Ecouen. It stood upon a great platform with battered sides, look-out turrets at the corners and a moat around it. The building itself was a vast quadrilateral with deeply projecting corner pavilions (corresponding to the corner towers of a fortified castle) and closed in front by a plain thick wall surmounted by a narrow balustraded terrace. All that remains of it today is the wing (less the corner pavilions) at the far end of the courtyard. The style of the outer façade is austere, the ornamentation being merely a number of small balconies carried on consoles. (The military note is emphasised by reproducing the medieval brattice in profile on the consoles.) In the middle of the front façade is a five-storey pavilion housing the great staircase with its two straight flights separated by a string-wall. Eight huge stone fireplaces inlaid with coloured marble and lavishly decorated with carvings of statues, trophies and armorial bearings have survived inside the château. The violent contrast between this exaggerated ornamentation and the bare austerity of the façades is explained by the fact that the architect, Pierre Souffron, who was in charge at the outset, left in 1603 before the main building was finished and cannot therefore be held responsible for the doubtful taste displayed in the style of the fireplaces.

The transformation of the fifteenth-century fortified castle at Brissac began in 1606 and went on until 1621. The general theme was the same as at Cadillac; but building was stopped when only one half of the main wing was completed, and even the round towers of the old castle were left standing. What was meant to be its main feature – as at Cadillac – was the great domed pavilion enclosing the straight, double staircase. The decoration of the outer façade is, however, quite different from that of Cadillac; it is lavishly ornamented in an incipiently Baroque style with stone linings around the windows, ringed pilasters, rounded bossages, niches, broken pediments and even (on the top floor of the large pavilion) superimposed pediments.

Vizille, which was built between 1611 and 1620, stands on a high plinth and gives the impression of a fortified castle with its round towers and its six-storey, square pavilion. Although the configuration of the site was unsuitable, an

xxvi *Flamanville*

effort was made to produce a more modern plan by creating
on the north side of the main wing a courtyard lined with
buildings on three sides and closed on the fourth side by a
plain wall and a monumental gateway. The north and east
sides of this courtyard were destroyed by fire in the nineteenth
century. All that has survived of the original building is,
first, the main (south) wing with its horseshoe staircase and
stone linings at the windows; and, second, the porch, which
with its bold, bossed columns and the statue of Lesdiguières
over the door is in the typically robust style of the period.
(See Plate xxii.)

The Luxembourg (in Paris) was built for Marie de Médicis
by Salomon de Brosse between 1615 and 1626. Like Vizille, it
follows the pattern of the sixteenth-century chateaux. It can
be shown that its main source of inspiration was Verneuil-sur-
Oise (since disappeared), which was designed by one of the
Du Cerceau family – probably the elder Jacques, author of
Les plus excellents bastimens de France. Salomon de Brosse, who
was born at Verneuil, was related to the Du Cerceau family
on his mother's side. Although the rusticated masonry of the
Luxembourg recalls the Pitti Palace in Florence, the Luxembourg, in all its main features, shows its close affinity to
Verneuil. It has the traditional quadrilateral plan with the
grand staircase in the middle of the rear wing; the façades are
surmounted by balustrades at the height of the gutters. The
similarity is even more marked in the front wing of the courtyard, which is composed of two three-storey pavilions connected by a long low gallery decorated with heavily rusticated
pilasters and covered by a terraced roof; in the middle of this
gallery is a domed pavilion.

Monumental gateways in the 'grand' style of that of the
Luxembourg were becoming a thing of the past. One other
example might, however, be mentioned at the old castle
once belonging to the Coligny family at Tanlay (Yonne) and
acquired later by Particelli d'Emery, who had it completed
and restored by Le Muet between 1643 and 1649. The
façades were lavishly adorned with pilasters – four between
each window – and a gateway pavilion was erected at the
centre of the low balustrade that encloses the front of the
courtyard. The pavilion is a massive structure decorated

with columns that have ringed corrugations from top to bottom. In front of the pavilion (to right and left of the entrance) are two tapering obelisks with similar corrugations. M. Louis Hautecœur has remarked that the whole structure reminds him of the gate of a walled city; its pseudo-military appearance is at least in keeping with the symbolic grenades carved on the chimney-stacks. (See Plate XXVII.)

4 | The Passing of the Court of Honour

In the course of time gateway pavilions came to be considered as outmoded and cumbersome;[1] it was felt, on the contrary, that the courtyard should be opened up to the fullest possible extent. A beginning was made by the simple operation of suppressing the front wing altogether and replacing it by a railing lining the moat. This was the plan adopted at Grosbois (near Paris), which has a number of interesting features well worth studying. (See Plate XXV.)

The estate was purchased by Charles de Valois, natural son of Charles IX and Marie Touchet, while he was still Count of Auvergne, that is to say, before January 1620, when he became Duc d'Angoulême. A château already existed at Grosbois, built in about 1580 by the former owner. According to M. Soulange-Bodin, the main building at the far end of the courtyard (which has an unusual, convex façade) was part of the original sixteenth-century château. It seems that it was Charles de Valois who built the four pavilions flanking this building and also the lateral wings of the court of honour with their two pavilions on the right and left of the entrance. This point, however, must be noted: although the whole building is in brick and stone it is not of the same style throughout. The wing at the far end of the courtyard is different in design from those erected by Charles de Valois, which are easily recognisable by the fact that all the upper floors have semi-dormer windows cut through the cornice. Openings of this kind – very similar to those of

---

[1] Jean le Laboureur, in his *Journal de Voyage*, in 1659, notes that a gateway pavilion had been planned for Cadillac but had been abandoned; and he adds, 'I think the plan was ill-conceived for it would have hidden and darkened the courtyard.'

Grosbois – may be seen at the abbatial palace of Saint-
Germain des-Près, built in 1586 by Cardinal de Bourbon.
They are found also on all the façades of the Châtelet at
Chantilly; and if one remembers that Charles de Valois' wife
was the daughter of Henri de Montmorency, Constable of
France and owner of Chantilly, it must be admitted that
some doubt exists as to the architectural parentage of Gros-
bois; it could have been either Saint-Germain-des-Près or
Chantilly.

There can be no doubt, in any case, that it is Renaissance in
origin, although it would be fair to add that it is not a servile
copy of the style. The architect was skilful enough to transform the traditional theme into a style of his own by creating
new combinations of brick and stone, using stone voussoirs, for
example, against a brick background, or outlining the windows in brick against a stone background.

Flamanville (Manche) was built between 1654 and 1658
(thirty years later than Grosbois) by Hervé Basan, the chief
judge of Cotentin. In spite of the somewhat archaic effect
produced by the small towers flanking the corner pavilions,
the building as a whole shows that an effort was made to
follow the prevailing style; it also shows that provincial
architects had been impressed by Le Muet's[1] 'Manière de
bien bastir'. In the second part of the 1647 edition of this
book Muet gives the plans and elevations of his own château
(now disappeared) of Pont-en-Champagne (Aube), to which
Flamanville bears a striking resemblance. It has the same
quadrilateral plan, corner pavilions and moat, the same
gallery forming one of the lateral wings and the same position
of the chapel in one of the front pavilions. The staircases
also are sited, as at Flamanville, in the angles of the courtyard in order to allow more space for the reception rooms
in the far wing; but, more especially, it has the same
double pavilions (one smaller than the other), although at
Flamanville these take the form of a shortened wing. (See
Plate XXVI.)

The building is of granite, and the decoration is necessarily
austere. The wide curved pediment covering the three centre

[1] Pierre le Muet (1591–1669)

windows of the main façade is in the contemporary style and can also be seen at Blérancourt and Cany. The dormers are very similar to those of the great Renaissance château at Kerjean, also built of granite; they continue the line of the windows up through the edge of the roof and have triangular pediments embellished with three vases covered with pebbles.

Blérancourt was built in 1614, many years before Flamanville. The architect, Salomon de Brosse, had opened up the court of honour by suppressing not only the front but also the lateral wings. The building was thus reduced to the château itself (now disappeared) standing on an open courtyard surrounded by a moat, with two corner pavilions and a central gateway at the front. It will be remembered, however, that this arrangement was not the first of its kind; it already existed in the middle of the sixteenth century at La Morinière. It is also seen at Balleroy in Normandy, built between 1626–36, where the château itself stands at the far end of a courtyard and two small corner pavilions guard the entrance. Although not built in brick and stone, Balleroy is often quoted as being characteristic of the Louis XIII style. The walls, however, are made of blue-purple shale, which gives colourful relief to the vertical lines of stone at the windows and corners of the building. The general plan is extremely simple, comprising three buildings of equal width each having three windows at each floor. The central building (which forms the principal motif) dominates the others by its extra storey, and is surmounted by a roof in the form of a truncated pyramid, and finally by a lantern. The only ornamentation is a carved vase crowning three of the dormers. Balleroy owes its distinction to the dignity and restraint of its style and to the care and skill devoted to ensuring the harmony of its proportions.

5 | Châteaux on the Massed Plan

It was becoming increasingly apparent that the small pavilions at the entrance to the court of honour of châteaux like Blérancourt and Balleroy would in time disappear and that the château of the future would be a small building standing on an open court surrounded by a moat. It is worth noting, incidentally, that once again the sixteenth century had anticipated a plan of this kind in such buildings as Madrid (near Paris) and Herbault (Loir-et-Cher).

One of the earliest châteaux of this type, built by the Gouffier family at Saint-Loup-sur-Thouet (Deux Sèvres) in the early years of the seventeenth century, has preserved all the graceful elegance of the Renaissance style. Although its plan has, in fact, the form of a horseshoe, the lateral wings are so short that they amount to little more than sharply projecting pavilions. Its general effect is enlivened by the number and variety of the separate roofs on each part of the building. Each window on the façades is flanked by stone piers rising from ground-level up to the gutters and surmounted above the windows by a small rounded pediment pierced with an *œil-de-bœuf*. M. Louis Hautecœur (*Histoire de l'architecture classique*, Chap. I, p. 772) notes that this arrangement was copied from Du Cerceau, but it is also an adaptation of the superimposed pilasters of earlier times. The austerity of the design gives added importance to the central pavilion, which contains the straight double staircase and is lavishly decorated with niches, broken pediments and cartouches. The denticulated pediment, however, has a sobering effect upon all this exuberance, and the building is finally crowned by an elegant campanile. The composition as a whole has much in common with that of the inner façade of Azay-le-Rideau, which is also richly decorated against a sombre background. As an example of good taste and skilful execution Saint-Loup-sur-Thouet should be considered one of the most attractive buildings of its time.

The reign of Louis XIII saw a notable increase in the number of châteaux on the massed plan. The two examples that follow have been chosen because they illustrate clearly the development of architectural ideas at the time.

Cheverny, which was completed in 1634, was designed by the architect, Jacques Bougier, a native of Blois. Its style is conventional in the sense that the principal motif is provided by the pavilion enclosing the great staircase, which has double, straight flights. The prevailing style was in fact

XXVII Tanlay

followed almost too slavishly, for its effect was to reduce the volume of the central pavilion and to give undue prominence to the two others, which were already accentuated by the quadrangular domes surmounting them.

To give the necessary modern note to the front façade the architect relied entirely upon his scheme of decoration. Instead of using separate compositions for each bay, as at Saint-Loup-sur-Thouet, he covered the façade from one end to the other with rusticated masonry interspersed with double string-courses, the object being to integrate the various portions of the building by means of a long series of horizontal lines. On this background the architect applied a generous scheme of decoration, comprising a number of oval niches with busts, voluted pediments and a mask and cartouche over the door. By due restraint in the manner of its execution he avoided what was an apparent tendency towards the Baroque in his composition.

In contrast to Cheverny, Cany (Seine-Maritime), built between 1640 and 1646, owes its distinction to the power and robust vigour of its design. The massive main building is flanked by two boldly projecting pavilions. The only central features are the great curved pediment covering the three middle bays and the great semicylindrical flight of steps in front of them. The ornamentation is very restrained, consisting only of simple pediments surmounting the windows. The effect is obtained entirely by the use of contrasting colours; the building is entirely of brick, but the piers are covered with roughcast, the brick showing through only as a frame to the windows and at the quoins. The whole composition is powerful and commands admiration by the amazing simplicity of the method and materials used.

CHAPTER FOUR

THE CLASSICAL PERIOD |

1 | François Mansart and Louis Le Vau

Most of the châteaux studied in the preceding chapter are conspicuous by their total disregard for the Classical style. At Brissac, Saint-Loup-sur-Thouet, or Cheverny, such Classical elements as are used are not only distorted but they are also reduced to insignificant ornamental details. Even at the Louvre, Jacques Lemercier paid no attention to the laws of Classical architecture, except when he was reproducing Pierre Lescot's façade. On the upper floor of the Pavillon de l'Horloge he deliberately subscribed to the heresy of superimposed pediments.

This lack of respect for the principles inherited from antiquity is implicit in the Baroque style; but a reaction against it was inevitable. The generation that came of age during the second quarter of the seventeenth century was more than ready to conform to the rules of Classical architecture and to re-learn its lessons at the feet of the Italian Renaissance masters; and particularly of Palladio. Of that generation the best-known are François Mansart (1598–1666) and Louis Le Vau (1612–70).

Two of the principal works of François Mansart, the southwest wing of the château of Blois and the entire château of Maisons, are still standing. Polychrome composition had become a thing of the past; stone is used throughout, and the whole effect is obtained by the play of light and shadow, the

138

use of sculpture being subordinated to the unity of the whole composition.

After the Montmorency rebellion, Gaston d'Orléans, having come to terms with his brother Louis XIII, withdrew to Blois and commissioned Mansart to rebuild the château. All that was done, in fact, was to rebuild the south-west wing at the far end of the courtyard. Work began early in 1635, but was suspended three years later and was never completed.

The importance attached in Classical architecture to the need for harmony as between each part of a building in order to achieve the unity of the whole could not be demonstrated more clearly or with greater force than by a comparative study of the two adjoining wings built respectively by Francis I and Gaston d'Orléans in the courtyard at Blois. The Francis I wing is weak in composition and, in spite of its massive cornice, would seem flat without the famous staircase tower, which was added later and gives it the necessary depth. The Mansart façade, on the contrary, is in every detail a minutely studied composition. The combination of the wide, projecting axial building with its truncated wings on either side gives movement to the whole. The smooth-shafted double pilasters decorating the walls would have made the façade appear as flat as that of the Francis I wing were it not for the bold relief given by the use of coupled columns at carefully selected points. On the ground floor these take the form of curved Doric colonnades in the corners to the right and left of the axial building, reminiscent of a similar motif designed by Salomon de Brosse for Coulommiers. Two pairs of similar Doric columns also flank the entrance; and this motif is repeated on the floor immediately above by two pairs of Ionic columns surmounted by a triangular pediment. This central motif is accentuated by recumbent statues on the triangular pediment on the first floor (in the Palladio manner), a large cartouche in the centre of a semicircular pediment on the upper floor, and by carved trophies to right and left of the pediment. It is finally crowned by a bust of Gaston d'Orléans. These sculptures were originally linked with the general decorative scheme of the façade by four statues (since disappeared) standing at each end of the colonnades on the ground floor.

The outer façade was never completed, but mention should be made of the magnificent interior staircase, of which only the well was actually built. Its plan was a complete departure from the Renaissance pattern of two parallel flights divided by a string wall. On the contrary, the steps of this monumental structure were intended to mount inside the huge quadrilateral well, which occupies the whole height of the building, although the steps themselves were to end at the first floor. Mansart, instead of continuing the walls of the well up to the roof, built a gallery round them at the height of the ceiling of the first floor, thus forming a large square opening through which the oval dome with the small lantern above it can be seen in true perspective from below. The whole of the upper part is richly decorated with sculptures of children and trophies. Messrs. Lesueur point out that the appearance of these sculptures in Louis XIII's time was significant in view of the wide use made later of sculptures of weapons and armour in the decoration of Versailles.

Maisons (now known as Maisons-Laffitte) was built between 1642 and 1650 for the immensely wealthy René de Longueil and was more fortunate than Blois in that the work on it was successfully completed. It stands, surrounded by a moat, on an attractive site overlooking the Seine and has much in common with Blois. It comprises a main building with a projecting central portion three bays in width, flanked by two deeply projecting pavilions. As at Blois, the various parts of the building have separate, tall roofs, those on the pavilions being in the form of truncated pyramids. The windows are surmounted by dripstones carried on elongated consoles, in the same style as those at Blois. The façades are decorated with two orders of pilasters, Doric on the ground floor and Ionic on the floor above. Movement is given to the façade on the garden by alternating windows and niches. Fluted columns are used at three points to accentuate the general design. First, the middle bay of the central building is framed with Ionic columns at the first floor, and (second) with Corinthian columns at the floor above. Thirdly – on the garden side – the ground floor of the two lateral pavilions is enlivened by small colonnades similar to those Le Vau was to use later on the façades of Versailles. The second floor of the central building is the dominant feature of the front façade; above it is a small square tower surmounted by a dome and lantern.

The scheme of decoration as a whole is elegant, but restrained. M. Louis Hautecœur has observed that the elements used (plumed helmets, trophies, etc.) are early examples of what was to be a constant feature of the Louis XIV style. The roofs are enlivened by tall chimney-stacks embellished with mascarons and by wrought-iron railings crowning the two pavilions. The most noteworthy feature inside the building is the famous grand staircase, built entirely in stone on the same square plan as at Blois; its broad, bare walls make a restful background to the sculptured figures of children grouped under the entablature.

A few years after Maisons had been completed, Superintendent Fouquet[1] – who was even more wealthy than René de Longueil – put in hand the building of Vaux-le-Vicomte, which he determined should be the most fabulous residence in France. He therefore enlisted the services of a brilliant team of young architects: Louis Le Vau, André Le Nôtre and Charles Le Brun – all three between forty and forty-five years of age. Work began in August 1656 and made rapid progress. Within a year the main fabric was finished, and the decoration itself was almost completed in time for the famous fête organised by Fouquet in honour of the King's visit on August 17th, 1661. Three weeks later, on September 5th, he was arrested.

The château stands on a broad terrace surrounded by a balustraded moat. Its plan shows a great advance upon that of Blois or Maisons. None of the rooms occupies the whole width of the main building, nor is there a central staircase cutting the building into two separate parts. The ground floor of the main building is divided in depth into two sets of reception rooms. The middle of the garden side is occupied by the great *salon* and from it to right and left, a series of rooms with communicating doors runs to the two extreme ends of the building. As all the reception rooms are on the

[1] Nicholas Fouquet (1615-80); finance minister to Louis XIV; amassed an immense fortune by dubious means; died in prison.

ground floor it sufficed to provide staircases of moderate size to give access to the living rooms on the upper floor. (See Plate xxvi.)

It is interesting to note that in Le Vau's original plan the whole building was to be in brick and stone, but this was modified later. The servants' quarters only are in brick, thus enhancing the white of the château itself, which is built entirely in stone.

Palladio's influence is manifest in a number of ways. The château stands on a plinth, which provides a semi-basement housing the kitchens, laundry, and other domestic offices. The use of massive pilasters on the corner pavilions is also characteristic of Palladio, as are the statues on the peristyles at the doors. On the front façade these statues are recumbent on the pediment; on the rear façade they stand upright on the entablature.

In his composition as a whole, however, Le Vau remains instinctively true to his French background. The varied designs of the tall roofs, for example, are entirely in the French tradition. M. Louis Hautecœur has drawn attention to the similarity between the façade on the courtyard and certain of François Mansart's work. Projecting features are used, for instance, in a manner very similar to that of the Chapelle des Minimes; and the small curved sections connecting the peristyle and the lateral pavilions are reminiscent of Blois. The pavilions on the garden side are surmounted by alternate œils-de-bœuf and grenades in a manner very similar to that of the château (now disappeared) of Coulommiers, where the œils-de-bœuf alternate with vases or statues. Le Vau lacks, nevertheless, the elegance of François Mansart. His peristyles, with their tamboured columns and over-size statues are too heavy; so also is the central dome on the garden side.

The principal reception room of Vaux-le-Vicomte is the great oval *salon*, which occupies the entire height of the building from ground level to the dome above it. Here again Palladio's influence is unmistakable, and one is immediately reminded of the Villa Rotonda at Vicenza. The decoration of the rooms and apartments was carried out under Le Brun's direction. The King's chamber and adjoining rooms on the

xxviii *Maisons, The Entrance Façade*

east side are enlivened with white stucco and gold, hence the
name 'the stucco apartments' by which they were once
known; the rooms on the west are decorated with still-life
paintings in the *trompe l'œil* manner.

2 | Le Vau and Versailles and the Louvre Colonnade

It will be remembered that after Fouquet's arrest his team of
architects (Le Vau, Le Nôtre and Le Brun) was taken over
by Louis XIV, and work was at once started on Versailles.
The modest brick-and-stone château built there by Louis
XIII between 1631 and 1634 was (like Cadillac) on a square
plan with deeply projecting corner pavilions. The front of
the courtyard was enclosed by an arcade, and the whole
building was surrounded (as at Ecouen) by a bastioned *fausse-
braie* and moat with two drawbridges, giving it a semblance of
a fortified place.

Le Vau set out to give the place a less forbidding air. He
modified the designs of the *fausse-braie* and of the ditches,
suppressing the bastioned redans and the drawbridges. In
1665 the courtyard (now the 'marble' courtyard) was
decorated with marble busts mounted on consoles.

This first programme of improvements to the castle was
completed in 1662 and 1663 by the erection of two wings of
servants' quarters and stables in the forecourt; but they were,
in fact, of secondary importance. The primary importance of
Versailles lay in the gardens that Le Nôtre himself was
engaged in planning. Versailles at that time was to be a stage
set for fabulous feasting and junketing in honour of the
King's mistresses: the 'Pleasures of the Enchanted Island'
for Mlle de La Vallière in 1664, the sumptuous fête of 1668
for Madame de Montespan.

As time went on Louis XIV succeeded in persuading
himself that Versailles was his own personal achievement. It
was not surprising, therefore, that he should wish to transform
his modest château into a huge palace. By the end of June,
1667, preliminary plans for further improvements had already
been prepared, but the King urged Le Vau to hurry on with

XXIX *Le Champ de Bataille, Central Pavillion of one of the Wings* the final plans, and work was begun during 1668. On October 11th, 1670 Le Vau died leaving his work unfinished; and it was under François d'Orbay that the building was finally completed.

It was Louis XIV's wish that the château his father had built should be preserved; but the ditches were filled in and three sides (excluding the front) were enclosed by new buildings. This explains the striking contrast between the front of the palace and the façade overlooking the gardens.

The front facing the entrance remained the old brick-and-stone residence of Louis XIII, enlarged by the stables and servants' quarters added in 1663, but also greatly embellished. The arcades, however, originally enclosing the courtyard were removed; a gilded wrought-iron balcony, supported on eight jasper columns, was added to the façade; the attic storeys were garlanded with gilded lead cordings; the court was paved with coloured marble around a central pool; and in the corners to right and left of the entrance were fountains surmounted by tall gilded aviaries. The general effect created was of fantasy and romance, described by M. Hautecœur in these somewhat lyrical terms: 'Brightly coloured stone finely laid; flashing fountains and the joyful glint of gold; and the ceaseless chatter of birds and murmuring waters.'

In contrast with the colour and movement of this façade the general design of the façades on the gardens is much quieter, and (for that time) strikingly new. The masonry was completed in 1671. There are three floors: a ground floor in the form of a completely rusticated basement pierced with round-arch bays; a 'main' floor decorated with an order of Ionic pilasters with their entablatures and enlivened at intervals with groups of four slightly-projecting columns surmounted by statues on the cornices of the entablature; and (finally) by an attic-storey crowned by a balustrade ornamented with vases and trophies, concealing the flat roof. (See Plate xxxix.)

Versailles as designed by Le Vau in 1668 was something very different from any of his previous work. It showed Le Vau in a completely new mood, undoubtedly under Italian influence, as is shown by the use of long horizontal lines and the suppression of the high roof. One cannot help noticing the resemblance between his new style at Versailles and Bernini's project for the Louvre in 1665, which also comprised a ground floor used as a plinth or basement, and a balustrade with statues at the height of the gutters.

The Italian influence is no less evident in the sumptuous interior decoration of the reception rooms, which had been planned by Le Vau but were carried out after his death. The walls are faced with coloured marble (quarried in France) and the ceilings with painted panels and gilded stucco.

Colbert – as is well known – was strongly opposed to the schemes for redecorating Versailles, and was far more anxious that the young king should concentrate on completing the rebuilding of the Louvre, which (in his view) was 'the most magnificent palace in the world'. During the early years of Louis XIV's reign the work there had been pressed on with some vigour. Le Vau built the south wing of the square court (which was completed in 1663) and began work on the east and north wings; but the question immediately arose as to the style to be adopted for the main façade of the palace, which faces the Church of Saint-Germain-l'Auxerrois. It will be remembered that Bernini was summoned to France, that he drew up the plans for a façade and that the first stone was laid on October 17th, 1665. Nothing further was done. The famous colonnade as we know it today was designed by a small committee consisting of Le Vau, Le Brun and Claude Perrault. This design was accepted by the King on May 14th, 1667, and the main fabric was completed in 1670. But thereafter the work hung fire. The King became increasingly obsessed with Versailles and less and less interested in the Louvre. In 1678 all work there was finally abandoned.

The Louvre colonnade, with its plinth-like ground floor and its balustrade concealing the roof, was a further example of Le Vau's later style.[1] Nevertheless it has often been criticised on the grounds that it is no more than an added decoration, making no positive contribution to the unity of the building as a whole.

[1] As the design for the colonnade was produced by a committee, it has often been asked who was the originator of it. Boileau, Sauval and d'Orbay thought it was Le Vau. Charles Perrault said it was his brother, Claude. The original project had been modified after the south wing of the square court had been doubled; and M. Louis Hautecœur thinks that it was this modified project that was the work of Claude Perrault.

3 | Hardouin-Mansart in the King's Service

The Treaty of Nijmegen was no sooner signed than Louis XIV began further alterations to the Versailles Le Vau had created. In collaboration with Le Brun, Hardouin-Mansart, who was thirty-two years old at this time, built the 'Galerie des Glaces' and the two adjoining rooms, the 'Salon de la Guerre' and 'Salon de la Paix'. The work, begun in 1678 and completed in 1686, was an architectural undertaking of major importance. The scheme of decoration was the same as that used by Le Vau for the reception rooms, that is to say, a combination of coloured marble, paintings, bronzes and gilded stucco. The marbles, however, were of less vivid colours – dull reds, pale greens and veined white – and the great attraction of this immense gallery were the panelled mirrors supplied from the State manufactory set up by Colbert. The whole of the arcades facing the windows were covered with these mirrors, giving a brilliant and novel lighting effect to the gallery.

The Galerie des Glaces and its annexes had just been completed when Hardouin-Mansart built the Grand Trianon (1687–88). This was the last of what might be called the 'gala' style of architecture characteristic of the early part of Louis XIV's reign at the time of Mlle de la Vallière and Madame de Montespan. The Grand Trianon is a one-floor building of which the façades are decorated in the similar manner to that of the Galerie des Glaces, with a series of arcades interspersed with Ionic pilasters. The effect is enlivened by the use of pink marble for the shafts of the pilasters and frieze and of white marble for the bases and capitals; the colour of the stone of the building provides a pleasing background. That the King had a predilection for the Italianate is evident in the open peristyle which leads from the court of honour into the garden.

It is somewhat surprising that the marble decoration on the façades of the Grand Trianon is noticeably absent from the interior of the building.

Since Colbert's death on September 6th, 1683, Le Brun's influence had begun steadily to decline. Hardouin-Mansart

– whose star was in the ascendant – was in process of renovating the interior decoration on lines very similar to those adopted by Philibert Delorme at Fontainebleau. No marble was permitted; no ornately panelled ceilings; no gilded stucco; even tapestries were forbidden. When, in about 1680, the private apartments at Versailles were being redecorated, Hardouin-Mansart covered the walls with painted panelling in white and gold. An example of his work at that time is still to be seen in Louis XIV's bedroom, which was then a reception room. The main theme is comprised of fluted and cabled pilasters with Corinthian-Composite capitals and ornate entablatures surmounted by an attic order. The architect makes lavish use of gilded ornamentation, and succeeds, by purely technical means, in preserving the desired impression of regal opulence.

Although the gilt has since disappeared, wood panellings were also used for the decoration of the walls of the Grand Trianon. In a few rooms (notably the great round *salon* and the study) the use of imbedded columns or pilasters still creates an air of pomp and grandeur; but in the Salon des Glaces these features are lacking. The whole room is covered with uninterrupted rows of arches surmounted by masques of women's smiling faces and panelled with mirrors in the same way as the Galerie des Glaces in the palace itself.

This scheme was improved upon later, in 1701, in the decoration of the King's antechamber – the famous 'Œil-de-Bœuf' room. Although, it is true, pilasters were still used, their shafts are more slender than those in the royal bedroom adjoining it. The 'mosaic' frieze, also, is enlivened by groups of children at play, and the wooden doors are finely carved with 'rich and delicate ornaments'.

This new use of wood panelling was, therefore, Hardouin-Mansart's creation. It was immensely popular, and in spite of changes in style it retained its vogue until the Ancien Régime came to an end. It can still be seen in châteaux and mansions in town and country throughout France.

4 | The Influence of Versailles

The influence of Versailles was particularly noticeable in the masonry of public buildings in France. Le Vau's ordinance for the façades overlooking the gardens undoubtedly influenced Hardouin-Mansart in his treatment of the Place des Victoires and the Place Vendôme in Paris; it was also the model for Jacques Gabriel when he built the Place Royale at Bordeaux. An even more striking resemblance to Le Vau's method was seen in the pavilion built at Fontainebleau by Ange-Jacques Gabriel at the corner of the Fountain Court. (See Plate xxxii.)

The glamour of Versailles also had its effect upon the castles and palaces of other ruling European princes. Although these lie outside the scope of this book an exception may justifiably be made for Lunéville, which is now in French territory. The château was built between 1703 and 1706 to the order of Duke Leopold of Lorraine by Boffrand, a pupil of Hardouin-Mansart. The entire house actually comprises two châteaux (the main building and the ducal apartments at right-angles to it) on a plan somewhat similar to that of the Grand Trianon. The wing containing the ducal apartments was, admittedly, added shortly after the main building had been completed, but it appears not to have been included in the original plans. At the Hofburg castle at Innsbruck a portrait of Duke Leopold (attributed to Pierre Gobert but, unfortunately, undated) shows a small painting of the Lunéville château backing the portrait. The view is of the garden (eastern) side, but the ducal apartments do not appear.[1]

The influence of Versailles is clearly evident in the larger of the two châteaux, particularly on the side facing the entrance. The approach is by two courtyards, each closed by a curved grill. The sides of the forecourt are lined with a row of independent buildings similar in their disposition to the wings occupied by the ministerial quarters at Versailles. The space between these two rows of buildings at Lunéville allows an uninterrupted view of the château, which forms a

[1] Our sincere thanks are due to Mr. Boris Lossky for having reported the existence of this portrait.

xxx *Dampierre, The Garden Façade*

horseshoe plan around the court of honour. The central portion of the main building has two floors, with round-arched windows on the ground floor and bay-windows on the floor above. All the windows have ornamented keystones. A cornice separates these two floors from an attic order surmounted by a balustrade running along the line of the gutters. The central feature of the building is provided by four massive columns forming three open bays through which the garden can be seen. Louis XIV had cherished a similar ambition at Versailles, but the structure of the old Louis XIII building was too weak to allow him to carry out his plan. It is abundantly clear, however, that Versailles served as the model for Lunéville. In both places the two courtyards are closed by curved grills; the buildings are similarly sited in échelon so as to carry the eye on to the central frontispiece; and in both places a balustrade follows the line of the gutters.

To give more life to his theme, however, Boffrand sought some means of introducing movement into it; and in doing so he went back nearly half a century, not to Hardouin-Mansart but to Hardouin's uncle, François. The lateral wings were made lower towards the front than at the far end, forming, as at Maisons, tiers of buildings at two different levels. Above all, the roofs were sharply outlined, each building having its separate roof; and the projecting central frontispiece was surmounted by a dome in the form of a truncated, octagonal pyramid.

Boffrand's evident inclination towards the picturesque is noticeably absent in the smaller château housing the ducal apartments. Its style is extremely simple throughout, and it has but one roof covering the whole building. Boffrand was obviously back, *in statu pupillari*, at the feet of his master, Hardouin-Mansart, the Mansart of Dampierre.

5 | Developments in style
Dampierre: Champs

It will have been noticed that the points in which Lunéville resembles Versailles are all located on the side facing the entrance, that is to say, the Marble Court, at Versailles and not in the building which encloses it on the other three sides.

The explanation is that by about 1700 Le Vau's second manner was already out of fashion so far as private building was concerned. Although Grancey (Côte-d'Or) for example, was surmounted by a balustrade ornamented with trophies, Grancey was an exception to the general rule. The Academy of Architecture, founded by Colbert in 1671, was reacting against spectacular styles in building and, in particular, it had condemned the terraced roof as being quite unsuitable for use in the French climate.

Hardouin-Mansart, who had been elected to the Academy in 1675, had built Dampierre (Seine-et-Oise) for the duc de Chevreuse in about 1680, and in so doing he had created in an ultra-modern building a completely new formula for a French château. (See Plate xxx.) It should be borne in mind, in studying Dampierre, that Hardouin-Mansart had just previously been engaged in modernising the old Versailles by the addition of the central frontispiece in the Marble Court and the wings for the King's Ministers in the forecourt. The points of similarity between Dampierre and Versailles are therefore easily understandable. At Dampierre, somewhat surprisingly, he used a facing of brick and stone, but in the reverse manner to that of Versailles, the stone serving as background to the brick designs. He followed the Versailles plan, again, in its alignment of buildings in echelon and in their disposition on each side of the forecourt; and, finally, by decorating the frontispiece on the court of honour with two orders of columns. Unlike Versailles, however, the ground floor of the lateral buildings is cut through by a series of arcades connecting the courtyard with the gardens beyond.

Once these points of similarity have been noted, however, it is clear that Dampierre has nothing of the ornate style or Italianate decoration of Le Vau. Hardouin-Mansart evidently insisted on preserving the moat round the castle, and even went so far as to flank the wings with turrets at their outer corners. The decoration of the façades, indeed, would have been restrained almost to a point of severity were it not relieved by the cheerful play of the brick on the stone background. Apart from the emphasis given by the two central projections (at the entrance and on the garden side) the only concession to ornamental effect is in the pediments over alternate windows on the first floor and in the alternating dormers and *œils-de-bœuf* on the attic storey. A vast, mansarded roof forms a symmetrical pattern over the building and gives the final effect of unity to the whole design; for the architect's guiding principle was clearly to produce a homogeneous composition and to eliminate all superfluous detail that might distract the eye and disturb the harmony of the whole composition.

The interior of the main building is divided longitudinally into two parts. For its decoration Hardouin-Mansart followed the scheme he had used for Versailles by panelling the rooms in white and gold. The main staircase, like the Queen's staircase at Versailles, has a square plan and is ornamented with marble pilasters and *trompe l'œil* vases (which were repainted in the nineteenth century). But, instead of the heavy marble balustrade, the handrail of the staircase is in light and elegant wrought iron.

Although, in general terms, Dampierre has much in common with Louis XIV's Versailles, it is nevertheless an amended version of it. In his *Histoire de l'architecture classique* (Chap. II, p. 597) M. Louis Hautecœur sums up the position very neatly by suggesting that 'Dampierre shows us what Versailles might have been if Mansart had not been forced to co-ordinate his designs with Le Vau's general plan'.

The sober, refined taste displayed by Hardouin-Mansart at Dampierre quickly found its supporters amongst the architects' fraternity in Paris. Another example of the Dampierre style soon appeared at Champs (Seine-et-Marne), which was built between 1703 and 1707 for Poisson de Bourvalais by Bullet de Chamblain, the son of Pierre Bullet, member of the Academy of Architecture.

Champs is built in stone and is surmounted by a large, mansarded attic storey. It stands at the far end of a forecourt enclosed laterally by two lines of walls pierced with arches masking the servants' quarters beyond. The front elevation (facing the entrance) is broken only by the deeply projecting corner pavilions; and the ornamentation is entirely limited to the central features on the front and on the garden side.

This motif on the front façade is supplied by two orders of columns and pilasters crowned with a pediment, very similar to the frontispiece on the château at Issy, built by the architect's father, Pierre Bullet. (This frontispiece was recently transported to the garden of the Rodin villa at Meudon.) The motif on the garden side takes the form of a curved frontispiece similar to that of Vaux-le-Vicomte, but without columns, dome or statues.

In one sense, however, Champs broke new ground in a direction that was to be followed by all eighteenth-century châteaux. The attention given to the internal comfort and amenities of the house was quite remarkable in a building of that period. By the use of small staircases and passages direct access was made possible to the bedrooms and other living quarters; the entresol was reserved to the domestic staff; and we know that several bathrooms were provided.

6 | Provincial Châteaux during the second half of the Reign of Louis XIV

Very few châteaux of the size and importance of Dampierre or Champs were built other than in the near neighbourhood of Versailles or Paris during the second half of Louis XIV's reign. The King's policy – as is well known – was to uproot the nobility from their provincial domains and to bring them under the personal control of the Sovereign. It was between 1678 and 1689 that the two huge wings were added to Versailles to provide living accommodation for the King's courtiers and their families.

A few châteaux were built in the provinces during this period, but not by members of the aristocratic families at Court. It is not surprising, therefore, that their style, on occasion, was somewhat antiquated.

One of the best-known examples is Champ-de-Bataille (Eure), built in 1680 for a member of the Créqui family. The château stands in a rectangular courtyard closed in front by a low wing pierced by the entrance gate. An unusual feature is that the courtyard is open at the far end, and the two main buildings face each other across it. The style throughout is of a past age: the masonry is of brick and stone[1] in the manner of the Henry IV or Louis XIII periods, the stone piers alternating with brick; the look-out turrets, capped with little domes, are reminiscent of Anet; and the balustraded frieze would have been more in keeping at Chenonceaux or Valençay in the first half of the sixteenth century. The central pavilions of each wing, with their four-sided domes, super-imposed pediments and massive proportions create an impression of the Baroque which must have seemed quite unorthodox at the end of the seventeenth century. (See Plate XXIX.)

Vayres (Gironde), even less known than Champ-de-Bataille, belonged to a local family (de Gourgues) and was originally a feudal castle rebuilt at the end of the sixteenth century by Louis de Foix, the architect who built the light-house at Cordouan (in the Gironde estuary). Under a contract dated July 23rd, 1695, the architect, Jacques Launay, was commissioned to rebuild the north-east façade. The plan included a new pavilion built on to the façade with a complicated system of steps running down to the Dordogne river below. This pavilion opens on to a wrought-iron balcony supported by eight columns with deeply grooved bossages arranged in groups of three and two somewhat similar to those at Vaux-le-Vicomte. The pavilion itself is a cube-shaped building with masonry entirely rusticated in accentuated horizontal lines. Fronting it is a porch composed of twin Doric pilasters surmounted by a pediment. A four-sided, bell-shaped dome crowns the building. The general effect is somewhat theatrical – in the early Le Vau style – and some thirty-five to forty years behind the contemporary style fashionable at Court.

The castle at Malle (Gironde) is built on a much more complex plan than Vayres. Its date is suggested by the armorial bearings of Lur-Saluces[2] on a pediment over the rear façade and over the fireplace in the vestibule. Alexandre de Lur-Saluces married Jeanne de Malle (the heiress to the property) in 1700. Following the prevailing mode, the forecourt was closed in front by a grille and lined on each side

---

[1] Described by the author as *en harpe*. See Plate XXV (Grosbois).
[2] 'Mi-parti de gueules à trois croissants d'argent et d'azur a trois fleurs de lys d'or.

by low buildings used for domestic services, and (in particular) for the storage of wine in this famous Bordeaux region. The court of honour at the far end is on a higher level and forms a terrace in front of the château. Two groups of steps lead up from the forecourt to the terrace and give added emphasis to the main building. This unusual form of approach is an attractive feature made possible by the fact that the château stands at the foot of a hill. M. Louis Hautecœur (*Histoire de l'architecture classique*, Chap. II, p. 116) quotes a similar arrangement at Lignières (Cher) built to François Le Vau's design in 1656.

Malle, which has a tiled roof, is a mere one-storey building in the form of a horseshoe. In its centre is a two-storey pavilion with a slate roof *à la Mansart*; at each end of the horseshoe are round towers surmounted by slate-covered domes. The chapel is in the usual position in one of these towers. It seems probable that Alexandre de Lur-Saluces merely renovated an older building. The two wings certainly seem very much out of date in 1700 with their massive towers, pointed, bell-shaped domes[1] and old casement windows. The first-floor windows of the towers are even cut through the base of the dome, becoming semi-dormers.

The central pavilion, however, was undoubtedly built by Lur-Saluces himself since his coat of arms appears (as we have said) on both the inside and the outside of the building. What is more, the dormers on the rear façade are decorated with the crescent, which is part of the coat of arms. The huge, smooth-shafted pilasters framing both façades of the pavilion are reminiscent of the frontispiece overlooking the Marble Court at Versailles, designed by Hardouin-Mansart in 1679; but the superimposed pediments on the ground and first floors, and the swagged grenades decorating the roof (like the vases at Vaux-le-Vicomte) are in an earlier, outmoded style.

No explanation has as yet been found for a curious feature to be seen on all the tiled roofs both of the château itself and of the outbuildings. Along the lower edge of each roof is a row of vases placed close together, forming a sort of ridge.

---

[1] *A l'impériale* (based on the ogee arch).

It is just possible that this ornament was inspired by the 'battlements' on the Foscari building at Gambarares as described by Palladio in the second book of his *Architettura*; but we make this suggestion with all due reserve.

Internally, Malle presents as confused a mixture of styles as the outside. The main building is divided, on a somewhat antiquated plan, into three rooms: a central vestibule, a reception-room, and a dining-room, each one occupying the whole width of the building. The vestibule, however, is decorated in the contemporary style with natural wood-panelling, fluted pilasters and handsome Louis XIV doors. The fireplaces are also of the period, the marble mantel-pieces being surmounted by a small attic order and (above it) by a painting framed in carved stone. On the ceilings, however, the beams are uncovered, except in the reception-room, which has small sunk coffers. The walls of a small room in the south-west corner of the castle are covered with pictures separated only by gilt beading. It would be wise, however, to ignore this anachronism, because it is our view that this work is not of the 1700 period; and it confirms our impression that Alexandre de Lur-Saluces merely rejuvenated an old château that was already standing when he married Jeanne de Malle.

Our comment upon Malle can in fact be summarised by repeating, in the first place, that it is the result of the restoration of an older building; and, secondly, that, unlike Champ-de-Bataille, it shows at least some attempt to adopt the new ideas in vogue at the time. But the local architect who built it was somewhat slow – or over-cautious – in following the prevailing fashion; and it is this fact which gives Malle an individual character and charm rarely found elsewhere.

7 | The Reign of Louis XV

Some fifteen years elapsed after the death of Louis XIV before any further building operations were undertaken by the Crown. The only royal buildings actually erected during this period were the stables at Chantilly (1719–35), which many writers consider the most important château of its time.

One of the consequences of the death of the 'Grand Monarque' was a relaxation of the strict control he had exercised over the nobility at the Court of Versailles. A new sense of freedom, and a growing interest in rural pursuits, led later to the building of a large number of châteaux during the eighteenth century.

Haroué (Lorraine) is, however, in no way typical of this period. Haroué was built by Boffrand at the beginning of the century for Prince Beauvau-Craon, whose wife was the mistress of Duke Leopold of Lorraine. It has many peculiarities. Its moat and corner towers are, in fact, survivals of an older castle built on the same foundations; but another remarkable feature is the sumptuously decorated court of honour, which has a central frontispiece of two orders of columns and a series of peristyles lining the two lateral wings.

This 'grand style' was a legacy of the seventeenth century, and was quite out of fashion in Louis XV's time, when all châteaux were, in varying degrees, modelled on the sober style of Champs. The horseshoe plan was still to be found in a few great houses such as Fontaine-Française (in Burgundy), built for the financier Saint-Julien between 1754 and 1758; but in general the lateral wings tended to disappear until all that remained were two slightly projecting pavilions merging into the general plan at each end of the castle.

Champlâtreux, in the 'Ile de France' at Epinay-Champlâtreux (Seine-et-Oise), was built for the Molé family in 1757 and is an excellent example of a stately home of France at the middle of the eighteenth century.

It is a six-sided building accentuated on the entrance façade by three very slightly projecting frontispieces, one at the centre and one at each end. The centre-piece is decorated with two orders of columns (Doric and Ionic) supporting a triangular pediment, and is surmounted by a dome formed by a truncated, quadrangular pyramid. The frontispieces at each end are decorated with a curved pediment but have neither pilasters nor columns. The windows in the three projecting portions are round-arched; elsewhere they are simple rectangles with a brace-ornament in the form of a female masque or console in the middle of the lintel. On the garden side the central frontispiece stands out in a bold

XXXII *Fontainebleau, Cour de la Fontaine*

curve, as at Champs. The Mansard roof is pierced with dormers.

Other châteaux built during Louis XV's reign were, in general, mere variations on this theme. Columns and pilasters tend to be thought pretentious and are used only as the central motif of a façade. In many cases they are dispensed with completely and the corners of projecting frontispieces are merely emphasised by rustication but never *en harpe* (see footnote [1] p. 153). The round-arched bay also becomes increasingly unpopular – on account of its pretentiousness – and gradually disappears, leaving only rectangular or carved lintels with a brace-ornament at the keystones.

Villarceaux (Seine-et-Oise), Omonville (Eure, see Plate XXXI), and Saint-Pierre-Eglise (Manche), built at about 1750, are good examples of this style. Another – and very attractive – example is at Bourg-Saint-Léonard (Orne), which was built between 1763 and 1767, for David Cromot, who was secretary to the King's Cabinet. Bourg-Saint-Léonard was contemporary with the Petit Trianon and of somewhat later date than the other three; which explains the presence of an Italianate balustrade at the height of the gutters.

In all these châteaux a pediment (usually triangular) was used to soften the lines of the central frontispiece, and at Bourg-Saint-Léonard and elsewhere the importance of this central motif was accentuated by the addition of a wrought-iron balcony. In some châteaux in the south, notably at Assas and L'Engarran near Montpellier (dated about 1760), the balcony was carried on telemones, following a practice common in the seventeenth century and brilliantly exemplified by Puget's[1] famous caryatids at Toulon.

At Le Marais (Seine-et-Oise), built during the last few years of Louis XV's reign, the ground-floor portion of the central frontispiece was opened up to form a loggia similar to that at Champs, with four sharply accentuated Doric columns. Note also the revival of a much earlier style in the bas-reliefs over the windows; they will recall Vaux-le-Vicomte, built more than a century before.

---

[1] Pierre Puget (1620–94), famous French sculptor.

XXXII *Compiègne*

8 | Small Apartments: Small Houses

In outward appearance, the châteaux of the Louis XV period give an impression of extreme restraint, if not of severity; and it is difficult to realise that this same period was the heyday of the Rococo style. The only visible sign of a changing mode was the appearance of wrought-iron balconies on the façades.

Internal decoration, however, was quite a different matter, and it was in this sector that the new style was being created. Between architecture in the strict sense and taste in interior decoration there was, however, agreement on at least one point: the pomp of majesty – the 'grand style' – was equally out of favour with both sides. The arrangement of private apartments in small rooms of an intimate character had its beginnings (as we have seen) at Champs; it now became the general rule. Nothing could illustrate this point more clearly that what was being done at Versailles. After the Salon d'Hercule had been completed (1729–36) and the Queen's Bedchamber remodelled (1735) in the main rooms of the palace no further major alteration was made from 1738 onwards until the end of the Ancien Régime, except the installation of the small private apartments of the King and of the Queen.

The decoration of these rooms was the natural development of the scheme adopted by Hardouin-Mansart in the last quarter of the seventeenth century for the private apartments and for the Grand Trianon. The walls were covered with carved wood panelling in white and gold; the ceilings were white; the fireplaces were low; and mirrors were mounted over fireplaces and built-in consoles. But all pilasters and cornices disappeared from the King's apartments, and the new decoration was entirely in the style we now call Louis Quinze.

It seems unnecessary to add that Versailles was by no means the pioneer of the new Rococo style. It had already been in existence for some considerable time before it made its appearance in the small apartments of Louis XV. Early traces of it are discernible in the sculptures over the door of the round drawing-room of the Grand Trianon; and, indeed, between 1735–40 when the small apartments at Versailles were being got ready, the famous 'singeries' or 'chinoiseries' were already enriching the elegant interiors of Chantilly and Champs with the clever and amusing paintings usually attributed to Christophe Huet.

The cult of the small apartment created a fashion for small châteaux or 'follies' as a further reaction against the 'grand style' in architecture.

Houses of this type were by no means novel at the time. A number of manor houses had been built for King Rene[1] at Chanzé, Reculée and other places in Anjou during the fifteenth century; and it was said that he found life more pleasant in them than in his great castles. The 'house of Sylvia'[2] at Chantilly was originally built in the seventeenth century and had just been rebuilt at the time of the historic visit made by Louis XIV to the Grand Condé in 1671. (It was on this occasion that Vatel, the Grand Condé's butler, committed suicide.) Apart from the octagonal drawing-room, added later by the Duc d'Aumale, the house stands today as it was in 1671. Four years later Louis XIV asked the young Hardouin-Mansart to build the small Château du Val at the end of the terrace at Saint Germain. He produced what was originally a simple one-storey building with round-arched bays and stone quoins, outwardly unpretentious but a model of its kind that was subsequently copied in many houses during the eighteenth century.

These miniature châteaux were usually built on the out-skirts of towns, and they made their appearance quite early in the century. M. Louis Hautecœur quotes a passage from Saint-Simon's Memoirs in 1707, which refer to them as 'a rather new fashion amongst the younger generation'. It was certainly adopted as readily in the provinces as in Paris. Vantoux, near Dijon, was built in 1704 for the judge Berbisey; and a number of country houses (known as 'Malouinières') were built near Saint-Malo by privateering merchant-adventurers of the town. Le Lupin dates from 1692; La

---

[1] René the Good' inherited the Kingdoms of Sicily and Aragon in 1434, but he never succeeded in taking possession of either domain.

[2] A somewhat legendary figure, presumed to belong to the Grand Condé's household; immortalised by Gerard de Nerval.

Chipaudière (now in the seaside suburb of Paramé) between 1710 and 1720; La Mettrie-aux-Houets in 1725; and many others. The remaining years of the eighteenth century saw a considerable growth in the number of small houses of this kind. L'Ermitage at Fontainebleau[1] and Le Butard, at La Celle-Saint-Cloud were built for Louis XV in 1749 and 1750 respectively. Both houses were designed by Ange-Jacques Gabriel, and are the first examples of the clean, unadorned style he was to adopt from then onwards; rectangular windows with no brace-ornaments; the only ornamentation is in the rusticated stone piers. A few years later, in 1777, Bélanger built Bagatelle (in the Bois de Boulogne) for the Comte d'Artois. This house – which was completed in three months – is perhaps the best known today of all the 'follies' of that time, although it was subjected to a number of unfortunate altera-tions in the nineteenth century. The original attic order covered only the central portion and had no balustrade; and the Doric columns at the entrance were originally sur-mounted by a round-arched window with no balcony.

It would be a mistake to assume that the building of 'follies' was the result of the passing whims of a few great noblemen. On the contrary, as their numbers increased all over France these smaller residences became the country houses of a new, moneyed class and particularly of trades-people. Reference has already been made to the *malouinières*. Another well-known 'folly', the Bagatelle at Abbeville, was built as early as 1753 for the cloth merchant, Van Robais. It is a brick-and-stone house, rather lavishly ornamented. La Piscine, near Montpellier, dated some twenty years later, is decorated in a restrained elegant style in striking contrast to Bagatelle. Its only ornamentation is its rusticated piers and two finely sculptured wall-pieces of hunting weapons.

During the second half of the century a large number of attractive country houses sprang up in the Bordeaux region. They were known as *chartreuses*, or small isolated dwellings consisting merely of a ground floor surmounted in some instances by a low attic-storey. As time went on the style of these *chartreuses* became less and less ornate. At Beycheville-

---

[1] Now in the Boulevard Magenta, Fontainebleau.

XXXIV *Petit Trianon, Lateral Façaed*

en-Médoc, however, built in 1757, this process had hardly begun. The house is larger and the balustrade along the whole façade is embellished with vases; the sloping sides of the central pediment are covered with voluted ornamentation; and the low main building is flanked at each end by slate-roofed pavilions towering two floors above it. Later, in 1760, at La Lignière, in the village of Labrède (Gironde), the balustrade is bare of vases and it covers only the central frontispiece, which is opened up into a loggia with three arches supported on Doric columns. The most attractive – and the least ornate – of all the *chartreuses*, however, is Bel-Air at Saint-Morillon (Gironde), probably built a few years after La Lignière. Bel-Air is an unpretentious building of modest size, with a tiled roof bordered with a *génoise*[1]; but it is enlivened by a small, central frontispiece consisting of three round-arched bays surmounted by a pediment. The spaces above the arches and the tympanum of the pediment are decorated with sculptures of branches and garlands, which are given added emphasis by the bare walls of the wings on either side.

This chapter would hardly be complete without some reference to Reynery, a 'folly' near Toulouse. Although little known, Reynery has several points of interest. In the first place, it was the country house of Count Guillaume du Barry, the 'official' husband of Madame du Barry. Count Guillaume acquired the property on February 26th, 1781, but some doubt exists as to whether he built it at that time or merely rejuvenated an existing building. But even if the walls were already standing in 1781 the place could not then be more than ten years old because the balustrades at the windows and their chamfered drip-stones are of the period of the Petit Trianon. From a photograph, Reynery gives the impression of being a typical Parisian house, with its semi-circular frontispiece, its upper balustrade and its rusticated façades; but in fact it has a particular feature that betrays its provincial origin; apart from the stone borders around the windows, the house is built entirely of brick.

Although it is not certain that Guillaume du Barry built

---

[1] Superimposed (round) tiles, set back from the edge of the roof.

XXXV *Benouville*

the main structure of this 'folly' we know that he was at least responsible for its interior decoration, which is still almost intact. It was in the latest style of the period and somewhat similar to the original treatment of Bagatelle. The statues of Mars and Venus have long since disappeared from their niches in the dining-room, but in the circular drawing-room the painted stuccos can still be seen in their original cream colour against a background of darker cream.

9 | Ange-Jacques Gabriel

Although Louis XV took a keen interest in the interior decoration of his apartments he initiated very few building operations during the first years of his reign. It was not until 1751 that he began to concern himself with the considerable task of rebuilding Compiègne.

Paris was reacting strongly at this time against the growing exaggeration of the Rococo style; and it was between 1749 and 1751 that M. de Vandières[1] made his historic journey to Italy in company with Soufflot and Cochin. We have already pointed out, however, that the Rococo style had little or no influence upon the decoration of French châteaux. Although Beychevelle or the Abbeville Bagatelle may have been rather more ornately decorated than other houses of their period they show no trace whatever of the German Rococo style. The most characteristic of all French châteaux of the Louis XV period is the octagonal pavilion of the Petit Trianon (1749–50), which shows sophisticated refinement in every detail: in the complex plan of the building, in the profiled brace-ornaments on the openings and in the sculptures of infant figures along the balustrade. But one must remember that the architect was Ange-Jacques Gabriel, who was to become one of the leading exponents of the Louis XVI style.

The rebuilding of Compiègne had already been planned in 1738. Work began there in about 1751, but it was not completed until 1786. The plans were drawn by Ange-Jacques Gabriel and he continued to direct operations until 1774.

---

[1] Brother of Madame de Pompadour, later became Marquis de Marigny.

He then handed over his plans to his successor, Le Dreux, who completed the work. Gabriel extended and remodelled the court of honour and added a large wing along the line of the old ramparts, at an angle to the court of honour and overlooking the park. (See Plate xxIII.)

Compiègne was one of the great royal palaces, and, therefore, Gabriel was free – and, indeed, it was his duty – to ignore any inhibitions as to the use of the 'grand' style. The two pavilions facing the Place du Palais and the frontispiece at the far end of the courtyard are decorated with a massive order either of pilasters or Ionic columns surmounting the ground floor, which forms a basement of rusticated masonry. (Gabriel must have had in mind the Place Royale at Bordeaux, which he had just finished building to designs prepared by his father.) But times had changed; the style is less ornate than at Bordeaux. Instead of round-arched bays, the ground-floor openings are simple rectangles; instead of light, wrought-iron, gilded balconies at the windows there are sturdy stone balustrades; and the Italianate balustrade along the top of all the façades is bare of vase or trophy.

M. Louis Hautecœur points out – and it is worth noting – that Gabriel's art was never static; it was constantly evolving towards a simpler and less pretentious style. The transition is plainly seen in Gabriel's treatment of the great façade overlooking the park. It so happens that Gabriel's plan for the central portion of this façade has been preserved (and has in fact been published by Count de Fels). According to this plan (which was modified later) the windows were to be embellished with brace-ornaments and surmounted by small sculptured garlands placed under the drip-stones, which were carried on consoles. Behind the pediment over the central porch the plan provided for an attic order surmounted by trophies. When the work was actually carried out, however, much of this ornamentation was omitted. The attic order and its trophies behind the pediment, the brace-ornaments and drip-stones disappeared, leaving only alternate garlands and small pediments over the windows.

Owing to its historical importance the Petit Trianon can hardly be included in the general category of 'small' houses. (See Plate xxxIV.) It is in reality a miniature château, more attractive in every way than Compiègne, and at the same time a striking demonstration of the versatility of Ange-Jacques Gabriel, who built it in 1763–64. It will be remembered that the octagonal Pavilion at Versailles, built by Gabriel thirteen or fourteen years earlier, was an outstanding example of the Louis XV style. In the Petit Trianon Gabriel was equally successful in giving expression to the prevailing revival of interest in the Classical style. Fortunately for him he had never been to Italy and had no pedantic nostalgia for the antique. His so-called 'revival of the Classical style' was in reality no more than a new interpretation of classical French architecture. (Gabriel's small attic storey with its square windows is a clear echo of Le Vau's Versailles.)

The extreme simplicity of the Petit Trianon is a measure of Gabriel's reaction against the Rococo. All sculptured ornament is banned; even the brace-ornaments over the openings are eliminated; and elegant wrought-iron balconies at the windows are replaced by stone balustrades. Curves, too, must go; so must the round arch; openings must be either square or rectangular. The only ornaments allowed on the façades are fluted Corinthian columns or pilasters. The whole art of Gabriel's composition lies in the remarkable harmony of its proportions. By these outwardly simple means (which were, in fact, the result of painstaking study) Gabriel succeeded in creating, at his first attempt, what we now call the Louis XVI style. M. Louis Hautecœur is fully justified in suggesting that it would more correctly be called the Gabriel style.

Although less marked than on the façades, the decoration of the apartments reflects Gabriel's constant concern for simplicity. This work, however, was not begun until 1765 and was completed in 1786. From 1761 until 1764 Ange-Jacques Gabriel had been engaged in redecorating the interior of Madame de Pompadour's house at Ménars, near Blois. Most of the rooms had been covered with tapestries, but the remainder were decorated by Gabriel with wood-panelling, a large part of which is still visible. The style of this panelling is too restrained to suggest any incipient signs of the Rococo. There are (it is true) a few rose garlands around the beading, a few rather shy curves in the mouldings, some small inverted volutes; but the theme as a whole clearly shows a desire to avoid complication, while at the same time it introduces a number of new ornaments such as incense-burners, floral crowns, groups of arrows, lyres and laurel branches.

The decoration of the Petit Trianon gives a clear indication of the steady development of Gabriel's style. The borders of the panels in the King's study are lightly profiled and ornamented with a shell. In the dining-room, however, the only ornamentation on the panels are pairs of inverted volutes, although on one panel there is a decorative spray of flowers and quivers very similar to one of the ornaments in the boudoir at Ménars. In the great drawing-room the reaction against the Rococo is complete; the sculptures of flowers, leaves and garlands are treated realistically and with great restraint. The background colour was originally of very pale sea-green; the sculptures in white are relieved by an occasional touch of gold. The changing style is also noticeable in the cornices; the drawing-room has a foliated frieze, but in the other rooms the cornice consists of a simple row of classical ornaments (modillions, ovolos, *rais de cœur*, etc.).

10 | The End of the Eighteenth Century

We have already noted the influence of the Petit Trianon upon the decoration of Reynery. Another somewhat clumsy imitation of it was made at Pignerolles, near Angers; but there is little evidence that the Petit Trianon had any direct effect upon the decoration of other châteaux at the time.

The revival of the Classical style was increasingly apparent during the last thirty years of the eighteenth century, but very few architects could interpret it with such elegant dignity as Gabriel. One of its leading protagonists was Soufflot, who had accompanied Marigny on his journeys through Italy from 1749 to 1751 and was the first French architect to visit the ruins of Paestum. When Marigny inherited Ménars after the death of Madame de Pompadour (on April 15th, 1764) he commissioned Soufflot to redecorate the house. One might have expected him to seize this opportunity of demonstrating the new style; in fact he did nothing of the kind. Ménars was a seventeenth-century building with rough-cast façades and openings outlined in stone. Gabriel had added two wings to the existing building and surmounted them with an Italianate balustrade. Soufflot suppressed the balustrade and replaced the flat roof by a high one (not for aesthetic reasons but merely to keep out the rain). He also doubled the size of the main building by adding a one-storey wing connecting it with the corner pavilions. All this amounted to very little in reality; and Soufflot's principal activity was in laying out the gardens, which, however, are outside the scope of this book.

During the last thirty years of the century the revival of the Classical style showed itself more particularly in a leaning towards the monumental theme. An order of massive pilasters would frequently be used in the decoration of the façades of great houses. The Corinthian Order is found, for example, at Belbeuf (near Rouen), built between 1765 and 1790, and at Kerlevenan, near Sarzeau (Morbihan), built in 1780; the west wing of Valençay was decorated with Ionic pilasters in about 1770. This use of giant pilasters was not, however, directly derived from antiquity but from Palladio, who was considered the supreme authority on architecture and an exponent of the system of the one huge order; he used it himself on the palaces of Valmarana and Porto.

Benouville (Calvados) was built between 1768 and 1775 by the Parisian architect, Ledoux. He, too, applied an order of high pilasters on the garden side of the château; but he decorated the entrance façade with a magnificent peristyle composed of eight immense Ionic columns, the four rear columns backing against the façade. In this case, however, Ledoux was not influenced by the Italian school. He modelled his composition on the frontispiece built by Gabriel in about 1755 on the façade of the Ecole Militaire, facing the Champ de Mars in Paris, which has an exactly similar arrangement of eight projecting columns. (See Plate xxxv)

Palladio's influence is clearly seen in the four Corinthian columns forming the porch at the top of the long straight, outer staircase leading up to the entrance at Kerlevenan.

But in this case it was Palladio's villas, not his gigantic ordinances, that were copied. We find the same motif fifteen or twenty years later in two small châteaux of the Directoire[1] period near Bordeaux: La Louvière, built between 1795 and 1799, and Château-Margaux, built in 1802. These two buildings are extremely attractive, very similar in character and entirely in the Palladio style. The ground floor forms the basement; the entrance – which is on the main floor – is reached by a long, straight stairway leading up to a peristyle composed of four Ionic columns. The interior decoration is strongly marked by the prevailing Classical style. It may well be, also, that Piranesi's engravings had some influence on the monumental treatment employed, both on the façades and inside the building, which, like the drawing-room and dining-room of the Marais, are decorated with pilasters and columns. Some of the larger reception-rooms are even adorned with colonnades. It is interesting to note, in this connection, that when the ballroom at Compiègne was decorated in a similar manner (in 1810) Percier and Fontaine had merely imitated Victor Louis's work in Richard Lenoir's house in Paris.

The staircase also plays an important part in creating an impression of grandeur and opulence at Châteaux-Margaux, as, indeed, it does in François Mansart's designs for Blois and Maisons. The staircases at Benouville, Belbeuf and Compiègne are no less remarkable; all are on the same general plan of three parallel flights up to a landing at the first half-storey, then making a complete turn up to the first-floor landing. Most of them have wrought-iron handrails, which make a graceful and pleasing contribution to the general theme without over-burdening it.

The emphasis given to sculpture in the interior decoration again shows the architect's concern to conform to the rules of the Classical school. One of the most typical examples is to be found in Bélanger's decoration of the dining-room at Maisons in the course of the work he carried out there for the Comte d'Artois from 1779 to 1781. Keeping in mind the ruins of Classical monuments, Bélanger banned colour of any

[1] From 1795 to 1799.

kind, and limited his scheme entirely to stone and stucco. The coffered ceiling is embellished with sculptures of suns, lyres and other ornaments; Corinthian pilasters adorn the walls, and between the pilasters are four niches with statues of Flora, Cérès, Pomona and Erigone; a group of life-size bacchantes over the monumental fireplace are seen winding garlands round a tripod.

Painted decoration is, however, sometimes found over doors in combination with stucco in high relief; Marie-Antoinette's boudoir at Fontainebleau, which dates from 1785, is a good example. Grisaille in the *trompe l'œil* manner is also used as an alternative to stucco, as in the music room at Fontainebleau (1785), and in the drawing-room at La Louvière. Unfortunately, the six panels representing 'Les Amours de Psyché', painted there by Lonsing in 1799, have been taken away.

Small-scale decoration in the 'Pompieian' mode seems far removed from sculptured ornamentation in the 'grand' style, but it has, nevertheless, its origins in the Classical age. It should be remembered, of course, that the use of 'grotesques' dated from the discovery of the Esquiline caves in Rome at the beginning of the sixteenth century and that it was Primaticcio who introduced them at Fontainebleau. French ornamentists in the seventeenth and eighteenth centuries undoubtedly owed much to Primaticcio's grotesques, which were therefore no novelty in the eighteenth century; but the recent discoveries at Herculanum justified their being considered as belonging to the Classical period. Two outstanding examples are, first, at Versailles on the panelling of the private apartments of Marie-Antoinette, and, in particular, of the gilt drawing-room (1783) with its sphinxes and tripods; and, second, the painted decoration in the Queen's boudoir at Fontainebleau (1785), which has gilded mouldings and coloured motifs on a background of silver.

The story of the great houses of the Ancien Régime may be said to conclude with the building of the very interesting château of Le Bouilh at Saint-André-de-Cubzac (Gironde).

As will be seen later, Le Bouilh was never completed. Its owner was Jean-Frédéric de La Tour du Pin-Gouvernet, commander-in-chief of the provinces of Aunis, Poitou and

XXXVI *Vaux-le-Vicomte, The Entrance Side*

Saintonge. Victor Louis, who had just finished building the Bordeaux opera (1775–80), was one of the greatest architects of his time, and the fact that it was he who rebuilt Le Bouilh gives the place an added interest. Several of Victor Louis' plans have been preserved in the archives of the City of Bordeaux (Recueil 19, Saint-André-de-Cubzac, 45, 47, 48 and 49), two of which are dated and signed 'at the château of Le Bouilh, November 13th, 1786. V. Louis'. Work there probably began almost immediately afterwards. Victor Louis subsequently returned to Paris, but letters dated February, March and April, 1787, to his colleague, Gabriel Durand, who was in charge of the operation at Le Bouilh, show that Louis was still exercising a degree of control there.

The work seems to have been pressed on with some vigour, for on April 4th, 1787, Louis writes to the effect that he is 'busy with the interior arrangements', and that 'the worthy Count hopes that the roof will be on by the end of the year'. In any case it had made considerable progress when, on August 4th, 1789, La Tour du Pin became Minister for War; and to avoid any suggestion that he was using public money for his personal benefit he ordered all work to stop. His orders were evidently carried out to the letter, for the capitals of the columns and pilasters on the façades were left un-finished, and so they remain today.

One of the drawings preserved in the archives at Bordeaux (Recueil 19, Saint-André-de-Cubzac, No. 45) shows the elevation of the whole project as approved by La Tour du Pin. There is a touch of magic in the composition, which com-prises a central portion with peristyle and rotunda open to the sky and a pavilion at each end. The peristyle was very much in fashion at the time, similar motifs having been added to the entrance at Compiègne and at the Hotel de Salm in Paris in 1786. But Louis, working from an accepted model, was able to produce a completely new type at Le Bouilh. He first replaced the door by a rotunda, then raised the peristyle from ground level to the height of the first floor on a basement pierced with arcades. The central rotunda thus formed a rounded projecting frontispiece which he proceeded to embellish with two enveloping flights of steps. M. Hautecœur records that Louis had already used this very elegant motif on the provincial administrative building at Besançon (which is now the Prefecture). Its origin, however, can be traced back many years and can still be seen in the seventeenth-century château at Cany (Seine Maritime).

All that actually materialised of Louis' original plans for Bouilh was the right-hand pavilion and the low wing adjoining it. The theme was based on Le Vau's Classical treatment of Versailles, of which Louis had a convenient example close at hand in the Place Royale at Bordeaux. The ground floor – used as a plinth – was pierced with arcades and surmounted by a loggia composed of giant Ionic columns carried through two storeys. The pediment was replaced by a balustrade in the Italian manner running along the base of the roof. Unlike that of the Bordeaux opera, which is sur-mounted by a line of statues, the balustrade at Bouilh was bare of all ornament.

As originally planned, the main entrance at Le Bouilh was to have a double stairway encircling the central rotunda. It was impracticable, however, to wait until the château was finished without making provision for some form of access to the building already completed. A second entrance was there-fore built at the end of the low wing adjoining the pavilion, and from the vestibule a staircase of about fifteen steps leads up to the reception-rooms above. Although necessarily short, this staircase is of monumental proportions and has much in common with that of the Bordeaux opera, having solid hand-rails and walls of rusticated stone. The most interesting of the rooms on the floor above is the former dining-room, where the original stucco decoration has been preserved with its garlanded frieze, its sculptures of ewers and dishes of fruit over the doors, and two niches; one framing an urn, the other a statue of one of the Muses.

The domestic services are housed in an imposing building at the end of the low wing, cleverly sited at right-angles to it so as to be hidden from the front view of the château. This building forms an arcaded hemicycle and is a modification of a design which Louis had made in 1765 for the forecourt of the castle at Warsaw. In the centre of the hemicycle is the chapel, which is in the modified Classical style characteristic of the Louis XVI period. The interior has two rows of Ionic columns dividing the nave from the side aisles, and a vaulted wooden roof. The general design is obviously borrowed from the Church of Saint-Philippe-du-Roule in Paris, which had just been built by Chalgrin between 1774 and 1784. The peristyle in front of the chapel is a reproduction of a typical small Greek temple, and has Doric columns with no bases. It will be remembered that Soufflot had visited Paestum in 1750 and that in the Doric Greek Order – as used at Paestum and on the Parthenon – the columns have no bases. This Order was introduced into France shortly before 1780 and was used on the pagoda at Chanteloup (Indre-et-Loire) and on the famous portal of the Couvent de la Charité in Paris.

The peristyle and the interior design of the chapel at Bouilh merit particular attention, for it might appear that something significantly new had been created. According to information given by Comte de Feuilhade de Chauvin (the present owner) the chapel, however, was a later addition built during the Empire or the Restoration; but Count de Feuilhade de Chauvin was unable to confirm his statement, and there is no reason to suppose that the chapel – even if of later date – was not built to Louis' plans. As has already been said, all work on Le Bouilh was suddenly suspended in August, 1789, and it is clear from the Diary of the Marquise de la Tour du Pin that no further work was done until the Directoire period (1795–99). Louis died on July 2nd, 1800, and it is therefore quite possible that the chapel was not built during his lifetime. It seems highly improbable, however, that his plans were not used when building was resumed, since Louis' plans for the chapel were certainly available and the chapel is the essential axis of the whole building.

It seems fair to assume, therefore, that the chapel at Le Bouilh was the work of Victor Louis himself. It was, in fact, the culminating achievement in the development of his own masterly style at a time when the Ancien Régime was nearing its end. Victor Louis has been described – perhaps rather carelessly – as the 'Gabriel of the Louis XVI era'; by which it was implied that his style was tainted with conservatism. The truth is that there was nothing conservative in Louis's art (nor in Gabriel's for that matter), for Louis always kept abreast of all contemporary developments in architectural styles. As a measure of his evolution over a period of some twenty years one need only compare his plans for the Warsaw palace (1766) with the austerity of the peristyle at Le Bouilh. In the one the ornamentation is excessive, still clinging to the Rococo;[1] the other is an expression of the authentic Classical style in its most uncompromising form.

[1] These plans were published in the catalogue of the Victor Louis exhibition at the Bordeaux library in 1958.

| THE AGE OF DECADENCE

1 | The Revolution and the Empire

During the period covered by the Revolution and the Empire (1789–1815) very few new châteaux were built and a considerable number were destroyed, either deliberately or as a result of the depredations caused by the Black Band gangs, who were still active even after the Restoration.

We have already mentioned two châteaux of this period: La Louvière (built during the Directoire) and Château-Margaux, built in 1802. They are representative of the very small number built at that time, and in style they all belong to the Louis XVI period.

Napoleon I was fully aware of the importance of stirring popular imagination (and enhancing his personal prestige) by building public monuments in the manner of the Caesars, such as the Temple de la Gloire (now the Madeleine), the Colonne Vendôme and the Arc du Carrousel; but he showed no desire to build châteaux or palaces for his own use and was content to occupy those already available: the Tuileries, Fontainebleau, Compiègne and Saint-Cloud.

Even La Malmaison itself was not a new building. When Josephine bought it, on April 21st, 1799, it was an old house dating back to 1622; a surprisingly out-of-date abode for a *merveilleuse*,[1] with its high, angular roofs, its two pavilions

---

[1] *Merveilleuse* – name given to the (feminine) leaders of fashion during the Empire.

and their quaint semi-dormer windows. Nevertheless, it was decided not to pull it down. On the contrary, Percier and Fontaine strengthened it by buttressing the walls with Doric pillars, which hid their real purpose by being surmounted by statues and vases. Two low wings were then added to right and left of the entrance side. The rear façades of these two wings are soberly decorated with empty niches and a small pediment pierced with an *œil-de-bœuf*. In front of the door is the famous green-and-gold veranda which (it is said) Napoleon cordially disliked; and small wonder, for it bears an unfortunate resemblance to a shop-front. On the whole, these few embellishments are somewhat unimpressive; they would be more appropriate to a town house than to a country residence.

The interior, however, was completely replanned and redecorated under Josephine's direction. The library was the only room left more or less intact; but it was redecorated in a style that was strikingly new by comparison with anything that had preceded it during the Ancien Régime. White or pale-coloured panelling was relegated to the past. The room was divided into three aisles by two arches carried on double mahogany columns standing on breast-high plinths, also of mahogany. The bare, white ceiling was replaced by three vaulted sections covered with paintings in the 'Pompeian' manner of Minerva and Apollo as a centre-piece, surrounded by olive branches, palm-leaves and a variety of other ornaments, including medallions in profile of Homer, Plato, Virgil, Dante and Voltaire.

Napoleon carried out no major structural additions to the great royal palaces; his interest was confined to replanning their rooms and apartments.

Fontainebleau was the Emperor's favourite residence. The Revolution had left the palace itself virtually intact, but all the furniture had been removed, which explains the fact that all the furniture seen there today is of the First Empire period, with the exception of a few pieces which were added later. From 1803 to 1808 (when it was transferred to Saint-Cyr) the French Military Academy had been accommodated in the palace; and it was apparently in 1808 that Napoleon put in hand the work necessary to adapt it for his personal use.

The series of small apartments on the ground floor and the State apartments on the first floor were completed in 1808 and 1809; but, on the whole, the new scheme of decoration, in Josephine's bedchamber and in the yellow drawing-room on the ground floor, for instance, consisted merely in covering the existing wood panels with silk. The Emperor's own bedroom, however, which was in the state apartments, was treated in a more lavish fashion with panels hung with medallions and symbols of victory. But a few vestiges still remain of the Louis XVI style in the garlands round the doors and in the marble fireplace proudly displaying the eagle of the Austrian Empire; nor is it possible to ignore the painful contrast between all this elegance and the somewhat frigid formalism of the Napoleonic theme.

At Compiègne – as at Fontainebleau – Napoleon concentrated his activities upon the interior, leaving the buildings untouched. His own bedroom, his library and the Empress's apartments were completely redecorated, with the result that Compiègne today provides the finest examples of the Empire style existing in any château in France.

According to M. Max Terrier, Josephine considered both Percier and Fontaine as 'people behind the times', and she insisted on their appointing Berthault as her architect. On November 10th, 1807, Napoleon approved Berthault's plans, which had previously been checked by Fontaine. The decoration of the door-panels plays an important part in the general scheme, and these are divided into roughly equal sections, each one carrying a circular, ornamental motif such as a rose, a crown, or a medallion. A number of pilasters adorn the walls, and their bare shafts are decorated with various motifs placed one above the other. The finest rooms, however, are the Empress's bedchamber and the Salon des Fleurs, which have round arches surmounting the doors and framing the mirrors. The spaces between the arches in the Salon des Fleurs are painted with Redouté flowers and in Josephine's bedroom with Girodet's 'Seasons'. It will be remembered that the magnificent ballroom, which is surrounded with a colonnade, was modelled on that of Richard Lenoir in Paris. It was completed on March 20th, 1810.

The Emperor's generals and statesmen followed their

master's example. Talleyrand at Valençay and Marshal Berthier at Grosbois redecorated existing buildings in the contemporary style, but they made no structural additions to them.

Both Valençay and Grosbois have kept the traditional great hall, dating from the Middle Ages. At Valençay, Talleyrand decorated it with large-scale pictures of Italian landscapes; at Grosbois Berthier preferred battle scenes. The furniture and decoration still survive in many of the rooms at Grosbois, the most interesting being the Marshal's bedroom, adorned with pictures in the 'Pompeian' manner of draped nymphs floating in the air.

2 | The Troubadour Style

The Troubadour style was an expression – in the architectural field – of the revived cult of the Middle Ages created by the writers and artists of the Romantic School.

It is hardly necessary to quote the many examples of this style to be seen as early as the reign of Louis XVI, in the planning of gardens. But it is interesting to record – as, in fact, M. Louis Hautecœur has done – that on December 2nd, 1804 (in the early days of the Empire), Percier and Fontaine themselves used the Troubadour style in setting the scene for one of the State ceremonies. On one of Isabey's illustrations for the *Livre du Sacre* (the Coronation Album), showing Napoleon arriving with Josephine at Notre-Dame, the front of the cathedral is dressed up for the occasion in a pseudo-Gothic disguise which is quite definitely in the Troubadour manner.

Three or four years later Chateaubriand acquired the property at La Vallée-aux-Loups, and on August 22nd, 1807, he began the task of beautifying what he called his 'cottage'. To the garden façade he added a porch of black marble columns and white marble caryatids. He goes on to describe how he adorned the other façade with what he called 'imitation battlements'; but, still undaunted, he proceeded to cut pointed arches in the wall and to adorn them with Flamboyant tracery. Finally he crowned the door with a

XXXVII *Pierrefonds*

wrought-iron balcony in a pattern of interlaced, pointed arches.

'I was evidently anticipating' (he writes[1]) 'the present craze for the Middle Ages.' His claim was certainly justified, for it was not until fifteen or twenty years later that the Troubadour style was used in any country houses.

The best known of these – to Parisians at least – is the Château de la Reine Blanche, which stands beside the small lakes at Commelles, in the southern part of the forest of Chantilly. A small fortified house with watch-towers at each corner had stood there since the fourteenth century. It was later transformed into a tannery, but was described (for some unaccountable reason) in the guide issued in 1787 under the title *Voyage pittoresque de la France*, as the 'château de la Reine Blanche'. The tannery was purchased on April 24th, 1825, by the Duc de Bourbon,[2] and on June 3rd of the same year he commissioned Victor Dubois to rebuild it as a hunting-lodge 'in the Gothic style', if possible with a belvedere.

The house was completed in 1826 and has survived in its original form. It is a good example of the Romantic-Troubadour style, drawing its inspiration from the Flamboyant Gothic, with its balustraded turrets, ogee arches and its façade embellished with a triple niche displaying statues of knights in armour.

By 1825, the Troubadour style had become remarkably popular, and examples of it could be seen in every part of the country. It was during this period that Madame Adelaide (the sister of Louis Philippe, who became king in 1830) built the château of Maumont (Puy-de-Dôme) in the medieval style, while Fontaine was rebuilding the neighbouring château of Randan (Puy-de-Dôme).

It was also about this time that Lamartine rebuilt his home at Saint-Point (Saone-et-Loire) along lines similar to those followed by Chateaubriand at La Vallée-aux-Loups. Saint-Point had been a gift to Lamartine from his father on the occasion of Lamartine's marriage in 1821. It was a somewhat nondescript building in rather dilapidated condition, with

[1] *Mémoires d'outre-tombe.* [2] Son of the Prince de Condé, who emigrated to Coblenz in 1792

XXXVIII *Vauvenargues*

M

four round-corner towers. Lamartine added a small crenellated porch surmounted by an ogee arch; the windows were
strengthened with transoms; the towers were surmounted by
rows of small arches imitating machicolations; and one of
the towers was pierced with arrow-loops curiously trefoiled
at each end. He also added a new pavilion with windows
ornamented with ogee hood-moulding; and, finally, he
surrounded the greater part of the building with a terrace
carried on three-centred arches and bordered with a balustrade carved out in a circular, quadrilobe pattern.

The Troubadour style, however, was destined to lose its
appeal when archaeological research showed that it was
based on a child-like ignorance of Gothic architecture. If,
however, the term 'Troubadour' is accepted as meaning a
fanciful interpretation of the Gothic, the restoration of
Pierrefonds by Viollet-le-Duc was undoubtedly an example –
although a somewhat tardy one – of the Troubadour style.
(See Plate xxxvii.) The castle had been dismantled under
Louis XIII but an appreciable part of the towers and keep was
still standing. The keep had originally housed the residential
quarters and, once the restoration of the castle had been
decided on, Napoleon III evidently planned to make at least
part of it into a residence for himself. In a letter from
Viollet-le-Duc dated February 8th, 1858 (published by M.
Louis Grodecki), he writes: 'I think I am carrying out His
Majesty's wishes in planning to restore only those parts that
can be made habitable . . . If the keep were rebuilt it would
look very attractive in the picturesque setting of the ruins.'

The work was put in hand at once, following a programme
set out in that letter, which provided for the rebuilding of the
keep and the two north-east towers, known as the Hector
and Godefroy de Bouillon towers. Three or four years later
the original scheme was extended to include all the towers
and curtains. It was extended even further between 1865 and
1870, a hundred men being kept constantly employed on the
site. What was finally achieved, therefore, was not the
restoration of an old ruined castle but a new Pierrefonds
conceived in the Troubadour style. Apart from the keep and
the square tower backing it, all the buildings enclosing the
courtyard, the galleries, balustrades, the great stairway and

the raised chapel are new. The whole of the interior decoration is also new. The great hall – known as the *Salle des Preuses* – in honour of the great ladies of the Court – has a barrel-vaulted roof and a huge fireplace decorated with nine statues representing the Empress and her ladies-in-waiting. All the rooms in the keep are covered with paintings, but the decoration of the Empress's bedroom in the Caesar Tower is most unusual. It has pointed vaulting, and the hood over the fireplace is decorated with what appears to be a Root of Jesse depicting the Knights of the Round Table. Monkeys, chimerae and other monstrous beasts leer wickedly from every corner of the room. The idea is obviously medieval, but the animals are not drawn from ancient models; they lack the lively spirit of the early French painters and sculptors.

It would be easy to ridicule Pierrefonds from the archaeologists' point of view; but we entirely agree with M. Louis Grodecki when he suggests that to condemn its interior decoration as archaeologically unsound is to beg the question. Viollet-le-Duc was using the Middle Ages as his theme, but he was not attempting any exact reproduction of its style. He gave his fertile imagination full rein and created – almost as a challenge to the pedantry of the Schools – the most notable expression of the Romantic movement existing in any building in France today.

3 | Eclecticism

The rebuilding of Pierrefonds was the signal for a very extensive movement towards the restoration of other French castles. These operations often involved such considerable additions and alterations that it is sometimes difficult to determine whether a particular castle has been merely restored or completely rebuilt. The following examples are taken at random from various parts of the country: Vigny (Seine-et-Oise), Martinvast (Manche), Bort (Haute Vienne), Jean-d'Heurs (Meuse), Bourlémont (Vosges). It is quite understandable that in all these places the architects were at pains to adapt the new buildings to the style of those already existing, whether Gothic (as at Martinvast), Flamboyant (as at Vigny), Renaissance (as at Bort and Bourlémont) or eighteenth century (as at Jean d'Heurs). The Second Empire and the Third Republic were not, however, periods of restoration only; a considerable number of new châteaux were built. But neither in the new buildings nor in the extensions to old ones was there any sign of the creation of a new style. This period in the history of French architecture has been described as 'Eclecticism'; it would equally well be described as the period of Sterility so far as the imaginative faculty was concerned. It was a time when French architects were burdened with a surfeit of learning that was stifling their inventive powers and turning them into little more than copyists.

For the most part they found their models in France; but they chose them from every possible period of French history.

The Middle Ages, however, were by now outmoded, and such imitations of it as one can find, for instance, at Kériolet (Finistère) or La Flocellière (Vendée) were in the late Gothic, that is to say, the Flamboyant style.

On the contrary, the Renaissance was very much in vogue, particularly the early Renaissance as expressed in the Châteaux de la Loire; and from one end of the country to another, from Vallière-en-Valois (which is a flagrant copy of Azay-le-Rideau) to Saint Roch (Tarn-et-Garonne) a crop of Renaissance ornamentation appeared in the form of turrets, lanterns and pedimented dormers.

Chantilly, however, is a somewhat exceptional example of this vogue for the Renaissance style. It was built by Daumet for the Duc d'Aumale between 1875 and 1882. Before the Revolution Chantilly included two adjoining châteaux. The larger one was built by Pierre Chambiges between 1527 and 1530 in the style of the Loire châteaux and transformed by Hardouin-Mansart at the end of the seventeenth century. The small château (already mentioned on p. 123) was built by Jean Bullant in the Classical-Renaissance style in about 1560. This one has survived, but the larger one was demolished during the Consulate,[1] and it was this château that the Duc d'Aumale decided to rebuild on its original foundations, but not in the early Renaissance style of the château

---

[1] 1799–1804.

formerly built by Pierre Chambiges. Instead – and quite understandably – he chose to repeat the Classical Renaissance style of the small château adjoining it. In carrying out this plan, however, Daumet, like other architects of his generation, drew freely upon every possible source of inspiration. The low front wing follows the sixteenth-century tradition; its balustrades, ornamented with the sarcophagus motif, are copied directly from Anet; the monumental entry with its central door is a copy of the Baptistry at Fontainebleau, dating only from Henry IV; the ringed columns flanking the entrance are copied from Philibert Delorme's design for the Tuileries; and the flat pediments with a central ornament over the dormers are distinctly reminiscent of Ecouen. Inside the building the coffered ceiling in the Galerie des Cerfs has the same pattern as that of the ballroom at Fontainebleau; the arch at the entrance to the staircase is typical of Palladio; and so it goes on. The Louis XIII style, with its gay and simple themes in brick and stone, was also much in favour and indeed it shared the honours with the Renaissance style in every part of the country, notably at Sceaux (rebuilt by the Duc de Trévise in 1856) at La Turmelière (Maine-et-Loire), and at Villersexel (Haute-Saone), which was built between 1883 and 1885.

The nineteenth-century imitators showed very little interest, however, in the early Classical, that is to say, the mid-eighteenth-century period. Franconville (Seine-et-Oise), which was built in 1877 in the south of the forest of Carnelles, was admittedly a copy of Maisons; but it is the only example of that style.

On the other hand, the later Classical style of the second half of the eighteenth century was much in favour. The Empress Eugénie was known to have a veritable cult for Marie Antoinette and the Louis XVI style- although it went no further than making a collection of furniture of that period. Baron de Schickler, however, outbid the Empress by building an eighteenth-century château at Bizy, near Vernon (Eure) in the exact style of the frontispiece on the courtyard at Compiègne. The masonry of the ground floor is rusticated in accentuated horizontal lines; above it is a massive Ionic order carried through two floors, of which the first has pedimented windows and the second is an attic-storey with *œils-de-bœuf* surmounted by garlands. Baron de Schickler undoubtedly created a lasting vogue for eighteenth-century architecture, which had hitherto been somewhat neglected. During the Third Republic it became one of the most popular styles, and its popularity lasted throughout the period between the First and Second World Wars. One of the best examples built at that time was Montbazon (Indre-et-Loire), which was a copy of Champlâtreux (Seine-et-Oise).

In the middle of the nineteenth century seaside villas began to make their first appearance on the French Riviera and on the Normandy coast. No particular style was discernible in the early buildings, although some were apparently intended to resemble châteaux. M. Louis Hautecœur quotes a letter from Mérimée[1] in 1856 referring to the fantastic châteaux, Moorish palaces and other villas erected by Englishmen at Cannes. Very soon, however, villas along the Channel coast adopted the rustic, half-timbered style of the Normandy manor-houses, which eventually spread to seaside resorts all over France, although some architects subjected it to considerable modification to bring it into line with regional styles. On occasion the historical process was reversed and châteaux were found to be copying certain features of the villa. Edmond Rostand's château, l'Arnaga, at Cambo (Basses-Pyrénées), for instance, was built in the style of a large Basque house.

It would seem that the château today is a type of building that belongs only to the past. The First World War put an end to the building of new châteaux and, with very rare exceptions, none has been built since. Financial considerations may well have been a determining factor, although a number of large villas appeared on the Riviera between the two wars. What is even more significant is that when Royan was rebuilt after the Second World War a few villas re-appeared. But both at Royan and in the south of France a lively new form of architecture emerged; a form resolutely opposed to any imitation of the past in its quest for new and original ideas.

One may well ask why the same attitude has not been

---

[1] Prosper Mérimée, novelist, member of the Académie Française.

xxxix *Versailles, The Façades overlooking the Gardens*

adopted in regard to the building of châteaux; and the answer seems to lie in certain factors of an intellectual order. For most of the present generation the idea of the château has such immediate historical associations that a 'modern' château would seem like an impoverished descendant of some famous ancestor. And they would be confirmed in this view by the nineteenth-century imitations, which are such devastating demonstrations of the superiority of the original over the copy. The introduction of *Son et Lumière* since 1952 has further accentuated the idea that a castle is essentially an ancient building; a place where history was made in days long ago. We must face the fact that in this present age a modern castle is an anachronism.

One wonders if the day will come when a château will be built on an entirely new formula (following the example of certain modern churches) and be recognised as the pioneer of an authentically new style. There are no signs of it as yet. There is surely something significant in the fact that Pablo Picasso, instead of designing a home of his own, installed himself in 1959 in the seventeenth-century château of Vauvenargues, near Aix-en-Provence. (See Plate xxxviii.) If an ultra-modern artist of the stature of Picasso can display so little interest in creating new architectural forms for the château of the future, who will be found to take up the challenge?

| BIBLIOGRAPHY

GENERAL

Du Colombier (Pierre), *Le château de France* (1960). Foville (Jean de) and Le Sourd (André), *Les châteaux de France* (1912). Grand (Roger), 'L'architecture militaire en Bretagne jusqu'à Vauban,' in *B.M.*, 1951 and 1952. Toy (Sidney), *A History of Fortification from 3000 B.C. to A.D. 1700* (London, 1955).

MIDDLE AGES

André-Michel (Robert), *Mélanges d'histoire et d'archéologie* (1920). Brutails (J. A.), *Précis d'archéologie du Moyen Age*, 2nd edition (1923). Clark (Geo. T.), *Medieval military Architecture in England* (London, 1884), 2 vol. Clerambault (E.-Gatian de), *Donjons romans de Touraine* (1905). Deschamps (Paul), *Le crac des chevaliers* (1934). Dieulafoy (Marcel), *Le Château-Gaillard et l'Architecture Militaire au XIIIe siècle* in *Mémoires de l'Académie des Inscriptions*, 1898, pp. 325–86. Dion (Adolphe de), 'Exploration des Châteaux du Vexin' in *B.M.* 1867; *Note sur les progrès de l'architecture militaire sous Philippe-Auguste* (1871). Drouyn (Léo), *La Guienne militaire* (1865), 2 vol. Enaud (François), *Les châteaux forts en France* (1958). Enlart (Camille), *Manuel d'archéologie française. Architecture militaire et navale*, 2nd edition by Jean Verrier (1932). Fossa (F. de), *Le châteaux historique de Vincennes* (1902), 2 vol. Grand (Roger), *Mélanges d'archéologie bretonne* (1921); 'Chateau de Josselin' in *P.M.* (1930); *Anjony* (1951); Pudon in *B.M.*, 1955. Labande (L.-H.), *Le palais des Papes* (1925), 2 vol. Lauzun (Ph.), *Châteaux gascons de la fin du XIIIe siècle* (1897); Château de Sainte-Mère in *B.M.*, 1911. Lecoy de la Marche, *Le roi René* (1875), 2 vol. Mortet (Victor), *Recueil de textes relatifs à l'histoire de l'architecture en France au Moyen Age* (1911). Pepin (Eugène), 'Chinon,' in *P.M.* (1925); Gisors, in *P.M.* (1939). Poux (Joseph), *La cité de Carcassonne* (1931), 2 vol. Rey (G.), *Monuments de l'architecture des Croisés en Syrie* (1871). Ritter (Raymond), *Châteaux, donjons et places fortes* (1953). Ruprich-Robert (V.), *L'architecture normande aux XIe et XIIe siècles*, 2 vol. Vallery-Radot (Jean), Loches, 2nd edition in *P.M.* (1954). Viollet-le-Duc, *Dictionnaire raisonné de l'architecture* (1854–69), 10 vol; *Le château de Pierrefonds*, 15th edition (1928). Grodecki (Louis), *Le châteaux de Pierrefonds*, (1957). Lefèvre-Pontalis (Eugene), *Le château de Coucy*, in *P.M.* (1913).

Abbreviations: *B.M.* = *Bulletin monumental.* *C.A.* = *Congrés archéologique.*
P.M. = *Petites monographies des grand edifices de la France.*

185

RENAISSANCE AND MODERN TIMES

Anciens (Les) châteaux de France, Paris, Contet, 1913–33, 14 series. ANDROUET DU CERCEAU (Jacques), *Le premier (–second) volume des plus excellents bastimens de France*, 1576–79, 2 vol. BANÉAT (Paul), *Le département d'Ille-et-Vilaine*, 1927–29, 4 vol. BON (Antoine), Châteaux du XVIIIe siècle dans la campagne montpelliéraine, in *C.A.*, 1950, pp. 123–39. BOYÉ (P.), *Les châteaux du roi Stanislas* (1910). BRAQUEHAYE (Ch.), *Les artistes du duc d'Epernon* (1897). CHIROL (Élisabeth), *Le château de Gaillon* (1952). CORDEY (Jean), *Vaux-le-Vicomte* (1924). DUCHESNE (H.-G.), *Le château de Bagatelle* (1909). DUFOURCQ (Norbert), *Le château de Poncé-sur-Loir* (1954). FAUCHIER-MAGNAN, *Les Dubarry* (1934). FELLS (Cte. de), *Ange-Jacques Gabriel* (1912). GANAY (Ernest de), *Châteaux de France*, 1948–53, 4 vol. GEBELIN (Fr.), *Châteaux de la Renaissance* (1927); *Châteaux de la Loire*, new edition (1957) HAUTECŒUR (Louis), *Histoire du Louvre*, 2nd edition (1947); *Histoire de, l'architecture classique en France*, 1943–57, 7 volumes. HEYDEN-REICH (L. H.), 'Leonardo da Vinci, architect of Francis I,' in *The Burlington Magazine*, 1952 pp. 277–85. LESUEUR (Fr.), *Ménars* (1912); *Châteaux de Blois* (1921). MACON (Gustave), *Chantilly et le Musée Condé* (1920). MÉRILLAU (Jacques-J.) *Châteaux en Gironde* (1956). NICOLAI (Alexandre), 'Le château du Bouilh,' in *Le magasin pittoresque*, 106th year. PALUSTRE (Léon), *La Renaissance en France*, 1879–89, 3vol. ROSTAND (André), 'Château de Flamanville,' in *Art de basse Normandie*, 1957, No. 7. ROY (Maurice), *Artistes et monuments de la Renaissance en France*, 1929–34, 2 vol. SOULANGE-BODIN (Henry), *Châteaux de Normandie* (1928–29), 2 vol.; *Châteaux du Maine et de l'Anjou* (1934); *Châteaux de Bourgogne* (1942); *Châteaux du Berri* (1946).

| INDEX

[Figures in *italics* indicate the *principal* references
to the Château concerned]

187

Printed in Great Britain by
Cox and Wyman Limited · London · Fakenham · Reading